STUDYING ORGANIZATIONAL SYMBOLISM: WHAT, HOW, WHY?

MICHAEL OWEN JONES
University of California, Los Angeles

Qualitative Research Methods
Volume 39

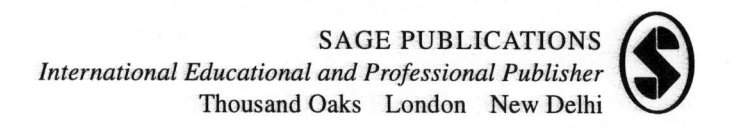

SAGE PUBLICATIONS
International Educational and Professional Publisher
Thousand Oaks   London   New Delhi

For information address:

SAGE Publications, Inc.
2455 Teller Road
Thousand Oaks, California 91320
E-mail: order@sagepub.com

6 Bonhill Street
London EC2A 4PU
United Kingdom

SAGE Publications, Inc.
M-32 Market
Greater Kailash I
New Delhi 110 048 India

Printed in the United States of America

Library of Congress Cataloging-in-Publication Data

Jones, Michael Owen.
    Studying organizational symbolism: what, how, why? / author, Michael Owen Jones.
        p. cm.—(Qualitative research methods series; v. 39)
    Includes bibliographical references.
    ISBN 0-7619-0219-8 (acid-free paper).—ISBN 0-7619-0220-1 (pbk.: acid-free paper)
    1. Organizational behavior.   2. Symbolism in organizations.
I. Title. II. Series.
HD58.7.J623   1996
302.3'5—dc20   95-50213

Sage Project Editor: Michèle Lingre

Sage Copy Editor: Gillian Dickens

CONTENTS

SERIES EDITORS' INTRODUCTION

Symbolism is about the production of meaning through the use of symbols. It involves the linking of a sign to a referent by some ordering principle. This process of coding (and decoding) is a mental and therefore a cultural activity. Symbols work to organize experience. In semiotic terms, they are signs that stand for something else. A symbol such as a corporate logo or a well-told joke may stand for a particular company or personal stance. Symbols also may invoke feelings of identification and honor or distance and absurdity. Symbols carry both denotative and connotative meanings. Denotative meanings refer to the direct, more or less instrumental uses of a symbol—the flag as representing a given country, a government building, a state holiday, and so forth. Connotative meanings refer to the expressive, broader uses of a symbol—the flag as standing for law and order, patriotism, national solidarity, and so on. To study symbolism is to learn how the meanings on which people base action are created, communicated, contested, and (occasionally) changed.

In the 39th volume of the **Sage Series on Qualitative Research Methods**, Michael Owen Jones looks specifically at how to go about locating, examining, and interpreting the symbols to be found within and across organizational settings. Specific techniques for analyzing (in always specified contexts) various symbolic domains of organizational life such as office architecture, workplace jargon, corridor art, and executive suite folktales are put forward systematically and illustrated by reference to numerous exemplary studies. Beyond its solid methodological advice, *Studying Organizational Symbolism* also offers a delightful look at the emotional landscape of work organizations, because trusted symbols have a power to attract as well as repel. Part inventory, part interpretation, part instruction, and part illustration, the intention of the volume is to encourage, guide, and display the kinds of research understandings made possible by treating symbolism as an elementary social process that makes organizational behavior both possible and meaningful.

—John Van Maanen
Peter K. Manning
Marc L. Miller

ACKNOWLEDGMENTS AND DEDICATION

I appreciate John Van Maanen's patience. He first asked me to prepare a volume for this series in 1988, pointing out that others do not focus on folklore. After several false starts, I set the work aside. In 1992, he inquired about my progress, noting that although the number of volumes in the series had doubled, there still was no guide to organizational symbolism and its documentation. Three years later, I finally submitted a draft to him.

That I completed this monograph owes much to Mary Jo Hatch, formerly a professor in the Department of Management at San Diego State University and now in the UK at the Cranfield School of Management, Cranfield University. She and I have worked on several projects together, including an essay on photocopier lore and a book in progress on the symbolic world of organizations; the present work uses some of the material I wrote for the first three chapters of that book. She has enlightened me about many facets of organizational theory and methods and has helped me understand the differences between a functionalist analysis (characteristic of most cultural studies and to which I seem to gravitate all too often) and an interpretive approach (which I now think is the essence of symbolic studies). Her insights appear directly at times in this monograph and always indirectly influenced its writing. Any shortcomings, of course, are my own. As the saying goes, "You can lead a horse to water. . . ."

I am grateful also to many students who, in the past decade, have taken directed studies, fieldwork, and organizational folklore classes from me in which they did research on workplace traditions. Their questions, data, and insights have contributed to this book, helping to structure it and illustrate points. I appreciate too, Jack Santino's permission to quote from his dissertation and the California Folklore's Society's permission to quote from Wendy Caesar's article in its journal, *Western Folklore*. Finally, I thank the series editors for their comments regarding which examples to shorten, what terms to define, how to better convey certain points, and so forth. Their suggestions helped considerably in my attempts to bring together from diverse sources a set of ideas about what organizational symbolism is, how it can be documented, and why it should be studied.

I dedicate this volume to the memory of two people who passed away in 1995 while I was writing it. Their work helped shape the two major paradigms informing research on organizational culture and symbolism.

Harrison M. Trice published extensively on rites, rituals, and ceremonials as cultural artifacts from a functionalist point of view. Barry A. Turner focused on the stylistic, affective, and aesthetic dimensions of organizational experience, advocating and helping articulate a symbolic interpretivist perspective. Their writings have influenced many, including me; I cite them and quote from them often.

STUDYING ORGANIZATIONAL SYMBOLISM
What, How, Why?

MICHAEL OWEN JONES
University of California, Los Angeles

1. WHAT IS ORGANIZATIONAL SYMBOLISM? HOW AND WHY STUDY IT?

Symbols are the most apparent and observable aspects of organizational life; simultaneously, symbolic behavior is the most subtle and elusive. On one hand, businesses, universities, and other organizations proclaim their identity in logos on stationery, newsletters, and even clothing (Dandridge, Mitroff, & Joyce, 1980). Many create slogans to inspire members (Peters & Waterman, 1982), devise rites of passage that mark promotion or retirement (Pondy, Frost, Morgan, & Dandridge, 1983), hold ceremonies to publicly reward employee service (Peters, 1978; Trice, 1993), and make heroes of those who epitomize organizational values (Deal & Kennedy, 1982). Few organization members or researchers fail to notice differences in the size of offices, quality of furnishings, parking assignments, and use of titles (e.g., Kanter, 1977; Morgan, 1986, pp. 176-177). When organizations seek to increase or reduce the effects of hierarchy, they target such emblems of rank (Raspa, 1989, p. 72). All these objects and activities are consciously, even self-consciously, symbolic.

1

Less obvious is that organization members narrate throughout the day about their experiences. Storytelling is symbolic behavior, because the accounts are not the events themselves but representations of them created by the narrators and audience through a process of communication, interaction, and feedback. Although the intentions of storytellers and the interpretations of listeners are not always easy for researchers to pin down, the narrating is clearly meaningful to participants; further, storytelling shapes the organization and members' understanding of it (Boje, 1991b; Hatch, 1993b; Schwartzman, 1989; Tommerup, 1993; Traweek, 1988). In addition to narrating, organization members participate in many other traditional expressive activities. They adopt the argot of their trade or jargon of their institution, use metaphors, joke with others, and celebrate someone's birthday or recent achievement (Jones, 1987). They personalize their workspace by displaying postcards, snapshots, photocopied cartoons, mementos, awards, or plaques (Dundes & Pagter, 1978; Scheiberg, 1990). They develop customary ways of carrying out tasks that become the "right" way to do things (Christensen, 1988). These behaviors are considered "the way we do things around here." Like the company logos and slogans, they are symbolic.

Both kinds of symbolization are appropriate subjects for research, although as a folklorist I dwell on the traditional, expressive forms that people manifest in their everyday interactions rather than focus on institutional symbols. Issues addressed throughout this volume are the following: What constitutes the database called organizational symbolism (in both its institutional and its folkloristic forms), how do you document and present it, and why study symbols, symbolism, and symbolic behavior in organizational settings?

Symbols and Symbolic Behavior: Definitions and Distinctions

Human beings, perhaps more than other animals, have a great propensity toward, dependency on, and responsiveness to symbols and symbolizing (e.g., Chapple & Coon, 1942, p. 481; Rose, 1962, p. 4; Rossi, 1980, p. 25; White, 1949). Cassirer (1944, p. 26) proposed that "instead of defining man as an animal *rationale,* we should define him as an animal *symbolicum*" (quoted in Schultz, 1994, p. 75). According to Cohen (1976, p. 23), "Symbols are objects, acts, relationships or linguistic formations that stand ambiguously for a multiplicity of meanings." Morgan, Frost, and Pondy (1983, pp. 4-5) further write that a symbol "is a sign which denotes something much greater than itself," embodying and representing a wider pattern of meaning:

> Symbols are created and recreated whenever human beings vest elements of their world with a pattern of meaning and significance which extends beyond its intrinsic content. Any object, action, event, utterance, concept or image offers itself as raw material for symbol creation, at any place, and at any time. (see also Goffman, 1959; Rose, 1962, p. 6; Rossi, 1980, p. 24; Whyte, 1961, p. 24)

Consider this example. On becoming head of the New York City Health Services Administration, Gordon Chase called in commissioners and senior managers. He asked them what they had been up to recently. Some told him how many meetings they had attended, the number of staff they had hired, the volume of memos they had written, and other bureaucratic activities they had completed. "But whom did you make healthy today (or last week, or last year)?" asked Chase. "Did you make anybody in New York healthier—and how do you know?" Chase wished to emphasize the results of services, not the mechanics of running public agencies. "I wanted the right perspective—I wanted my managers to be conscious of the fact that we were there to make people healthier, and not to lose sight of that fact in the daily squabblings that we all had to endure." The agency's mission, according to Chase, was to "make government work" by serving people and doing it well (Chase & Reveal, 1983, pp. 177-179).

To convey his conception of organizational values, Chase used language, a form of symbolization; that is, words stand for things but are not the things themselves. In addition, Chase's questions meant something other than what they at first seemed to signify; he was not in fact soliciting a report but expressing dissatisfaction with existing assumptions and setting forth new rules for behavior. He communicated this not through words alone but through the order of his queries, the repetition of his performance with each senior manager, and the fact that as the new head of the agency, anything he said or did in such circumstances could be considered a signal of changing values and expectations. Utterances, events, and conditions served as vehicles of symbolic communication and interaction for Chase on this occasion. The symbolic cuts through the "noise" of all the visual, aural, and other stimuli to indicate what is important and meaningful.

Symbols and symbolic behavior evoke emotions (Cohen, 1976, p. 23). For instance, Hirschhorn (1988, pp. 247-248) reports meeting with the representative of a research organization who had been delegated to ask him to facilitate a retreat for senior scientists. She told him that the scientists "felt undersupported and unappreciated and believed that the controller and president were 'nickel-and-diming' the labs to death. She thought the retreat would be a difficult one." Hirschhorn inquired about preparations and was told that everyone was being asked to bring a brown-bag lunch. "Having heard that the major presenting complaint [the ostensible issue or problem] was 'nickel-and-diming,' I urged her to tell the president that it would be better to provide lunch for the retreat." He reminded the representative that participants had to do difficult and emotional work; "they would appreciate such a symbol of support," he said. She hesitated, contending that the president might never agree. "Puzzled and irritated, I realized that I was experiencing the same feelings that bothered the scientists of the company," writes Hirschhorn. "So the president, even before I met him and before I even had a contract, was nickel-and-diming me to death as well!" Although trained in psychodynamics, Hirschhorn was not immune to the impact of symbolism. Use of the traditional expressions "brown bag it" and "nickel-and-diming" immediately aroused his emotions and colored his perceptions.

Symbolism not only affects how people perceive events, but it also influences actions. Berg and Kreiner (1990) argue that corporate architecture symbolically conditions organization members' behavior: "Churches elicit religious behaviour even in people who are not religious. Likewise, clean rest-rooms have been claimed to elicit tidier behaviour amongst users. Moving from the conference table to the easy-chairs in the executive suite often produces less formal interaction" (p. 46; see also Forrest, 1988, pp. 116-159; Larsen & Schultz, 1990; Morgan, 1986, p. 177; Witkin, 1990a). To illustrate the relationship between architecture and management philosophy, Berg and Kreiner mention a West German insurance company's building; the company president ordered a staircase design to, in his words, "encourage ambition and provide a visual image of our organizational structure" (p. 52). This contrasts with a Swedish company's flat design for headquarters; the lack of pinnacles and towers expresses an egalitarian philosophy and, in its symbolic capacity, is intended to discourage behavior toward hierarchy.

The symbolic may act upon opinions and beliefs. Martin and Powers (1983, pp. 101-102) report on experiments in which subjects were informed of a company's policy asking employees to take a temporary 10% cut in pay during economic downturns in order for the organization to avoid mass layoffs. Some subjects were given a story regarding the policy, but others received numerical data supporting or disconfirming it. The subjects presented with the story proved far more likely to believe the policy statement, to predict that mass layoffs would be avoided, and to identify with and be committed to the organization (see also Kunda, 1992; Van Maanen & Kunda, 1989).

The terms *symbol* and *symbolism* are common in the organizational literature; symbolic (or expressive) behavior is used in folkloristics. Symbol usually connotes something concrete, either an object or a behavior that is reified and treated as a discreet entity. Symbolism refers to both the practice of investing things with meanings and a "system" of symbols. *Symbolic behavior* directs attention toward people's interaction and communication in the course of which they generate, convey, and infer meanings and significance. *Symbolization* and *the symbolic* refer more broadly to the subject of study.

Symbols and symbolic behavior take many forms. Below are frequently mentioned categories (see Dandridge et al., 1980; Ott, 1989, pp. 21-38; Schultz, 1994, pp. 82-89). They are called *genres* by folklorists, a term of literary origin with aesthetic overtones, and *artifacts* by many organizational culture scholars, particularly those who accept certain tenets of positivism and functionalism.

Verbal Expressions

Jargon, argot, memos (their style and language)
Proverbs, traditional sayings, slogans, pet phrases, metaphors
Nicknames for people, equipment
Legends, cautionary tales, personal experience narratives
Jokes, humorous anecdotes, jests, numskull stories
Beliefs, superstitions, rumors
Rhymes, poetry, songs
Ceremonial speech, oratory

Activities

Play, recreation, games
Practical jokes, initiation pranks
Celebrations, festive events, parties
Gestures
Food sharing
Rituals, rites of passage

Staff meetings, retreats, ceremonies
Customs, social routines
Conventionalized techniques for doing a job

Objects

Architecture, design of workspace, office furnishings
The quality and allocation of equipment
Organization charts, manuals, newsletters
Bulletin boards (location, contents, aesthetics)
Posters, photographs, memorabilia on display
Costume, company uniforms, standard attire
Personal items made at work ("homers" or "government jobs")
Decoration of one's workspace or equipment
Graffiti
Photocopier lore (creation, collection, display, transmission to others)

This list assumes that, although any object or act may be treated at any time by an individual or group as embodying meaning greater than its intrinsic content, broad categories of symbols and symbolic behavior pervade human life. Studies by folklorists, anthropologists, and sociologists over the past two centuries have led to the conclusion that people worldwide and through recorded time narrate, play, make decorative objects, celebrate, ritualize, versify, and use figurative language (which has stimulated the coining of *homo narrans, homo ludens, homo faber, homo festivus,* etc. to refer to the human species). Research on organizational symbolism both accepts and confirms this conclusion. Documentation provides subclassifications of genres as well as examples of the symbolic. Researchers have identified dozens of narratives: myths, legends, tall tales, cautionary tales, formula tales, anecdotes, jokes, memorates, fabulates, personal experience narratives, and so on (see Brunvand, 1978; Georges & Jones, 1995; Nickerson, 1976; Stahl, 1977, 1989; Toelken, 1979). They have identified organizational rites of passage and have differentiated among rituals of enhancement, degradation, conflict reduction, and so forth (Beyer & Trice, 1988; Moch & Huff, 1982, 1983; Moore, 1988; Trice & Beyer, 1984, 1992).

Reference to genres of expressive behavior is important in a symbolic interpretive approach to organizational research because it identifies and helps us look for and at kinds of behavior that are known to carry meanings.

One danger, however, is the temptation to make concrete items out of dynamic processes of communication and interaction. Rather than thinking in terms of discreet entities (stories, rituals, proverbs, symbols, artifacts)— as this list and much of the literature on organizational culture and symbolism prompt us to do—we should approach the subject as behavioral and generative. During "narrating," for example, a speaker communicates not only through linguistic channels (words) but also through paralinguistic and kinesic ones (intonation, change in pitch, body language). Moreover, the speaker responds to listener feedback by digressing, explaining, repeating, emphasizing, elaborating, abbreviating, dramatizing, and so on (Bauman, 1986; Georges, 1969, 1979, 1981, 1987, 1990). Participants in a narrating event infer multiple, even quite different meanings from the varied cues; much depends on their experiences, feelings, and concerns in the present circumstances (the situational context that makes this narrating a "situated event"). Therefore, it is misleading to refer to "a story" or "the story" as if it has an independent existence. It is inadequate to document "stories" as linguistic entities with no regard for other channels of communication that convey information and affect responses. And it is misguided to assume that the event has a single meaning for participants.

Instruments as Symbols and the Instrumentality of Symbolism

Perhaps because complex events and behaviors have been reduced to isolated entities, the symbolic often is trivialized. To many, it connotes superficiality rather than substance (as in "that's just symbolic"). Structure, technology, information systems, and so forth are considered imminently practical—the nuts and bolts of organizational design and administration.

Structure, however, grows out of and expresses assumptions about the relationship between the organization and its members (e.g., a pyramidal hierarchy with a system of controls versus a "flat" structure). Who is rewarded, when, and why indicate what is valued in the organization. The allocation of resources is based on beliefs about who needs (or should have) what and in turn represents and reinforces those opinions. As Witkin (1990b) writes, although the work process is designed instrumentally to achieve certain ends, in the process of structuring action

> the organization must continuously revivify and recreate itself as a dynamic "agency" . . . . The work gets done by living actors who address each other in certain ways, observe certain niceties and rules of office etiquette and shape

their encounters, relations and actions in ways designed to reinforce and revivify the "organizational process" so that it is capable of delivering the action demanded in particular situations. (pp. 191-192)

Although recurring patterns of action may be instrumental, they are also symbolic and can be viewed as "styles" of action, "sensuously patterned, to realize (and express) *values intrinsic to the organizational process itself*" (see also Prasad, 1993).

A study of personnel departments by Trice, Belasco, and Alutto (1969; all quotes below are from pp. 44-49) helps make it clear that the technological aspects of organizations are symbolic. The office of personnel director may be legitimating for some as the repository of "scientific" information. "Organizational members appear to reason, 'If the specialist approves an action, the approval is justified on scientific grounds; and if a change is scientifically correct, it should be accepted by all concerned.' " This office's participation in new programs can symbolize "a corporate-wide approval of organizational changes." Personnel administrators appear to symbolize more general, societal concerns in that they are the official "keeper[s] of the corporate conscience" regarding fair and just treatment of organizational members. The presence of personnel administrators during critical periods such as hiring, evaluation, training, promotion, and dismissal can symbolize their vital role in these activities. Elaborate testing and interviewing of prospective employees is symbolic, because such extensive selection procedures may be inferred by both applicants and those currently employed to mean that membership in the organization is valuable. "Many managerial and supervisory training programs actually constitute effective rites of passage," as seen in the fact that some candidates receive a battery of screening tests; the selected few then are placed in isolated training units, and those who pass have their new status publicly recognized in an induction ceremony. "Attendance at training sessions, formal memos, telephone calls, and certificates are all visible symbols of the trainee's importance." Job evaluation procedures used to resolve questions about wage and other reward differentials are symbols, too. "The main organizational value of job evaluation lies not in its ability to precisely weigh jobs, but rather in its 'scientific sounding' approach to this problem" (see pp. 44-49).

In addition to organizational structure and processes being symbolic, symbolism itself is instrumental (Schwartzman, 1989, 1993, pp. 38-40). Numerous studies posit "functions" of symbolic behavior, such as its role in educating new members of a group (Louis, 1980), framing and making sense of experience (Van Maanen & Barley, 1984), validating norms for behavior (Ulrich, 1984; Wilkins, 1984), creating a sense of community (Arora, 1988; Tommerup, 1990), challenging social structure or maintaining cohesion (Nickerson, 1976, 1990; Santino, 1990), mitigating organizational contradictions (Scheid-Cook, 1988), expressing emotions (Harris & Sutton, 1986; Henry, 1988; Narváez, 1990), and providing escape through fantasy (Noon & Delbridge, 1993; Wilson, 1988).

The implication of all this, according to Morgan et al. (1983, p. 31), is that

> every topic which the organizational researcher studies has a symbolic aspect of some kind. Whether approaching the study of leadership, motivation, communication, control, politics and power, organization structure or change, or whatever, symbolic processes are at work [and] need to be taken into account. (see also Daft, 1983; Jones, 1994)

In sum, the instrumental and the symbolic are interrelated; objects and actions suggest meaning, and meaning informs the production of objects and activity.

The Symbolic in Relation to Folklore and Culture

In 1846, the Englishman William John Thoms coined the Anglo-Saxon compound *folk-lore* ("a kindred people" + "that which is taught": instruction, wisdom, counsel). He intended it to replace "popular antiquities," in vogue since the previous century. In proposing the word *folklore,* Thoms gave a collective name to a group's expressive behaviors rooted in the past ("the manners, customs, observances, superstitions, ballads, proverbs, &c., of the olden time"; Thoms, 1965, p. 5). Among other designations are "oral traditions" (used since 1777), the French *traditions populaires,* the German *Volkskunde* ("knowledge of the common people," coined in 1806), and the Swedish *folksliv* ("folklife," used since 1847).

The word *folklore* has come to denote (a) expressive or symbolic behaviors that (b) people learn, teach, and use or display in informal, face-to-face interactions and that (c) are judged to be traditional because they are based on known precedents or models and serve as evidence of continuities and consistencies through time and space in human knowledge, beliefs, and behaviors (Georges & Jones, 1995).

For example, the proverbial expressions "Attack the problem, not the person," "If you want people to tell you the truth, then don't shoot the messenger," and "If you want to get to know someone, walk a mile in their shoes" are well-known and often employed in organizational contexts (for their use by one director to express management philosophy, see Jones, 1987, p. 144). They are symbolic; we do not literally beat up someone who encounters a problem, murder the bearer of bad tidings, or don another's apparel. These expressions are learned from hearing others use them and are perpetuated through oral communication. This is the essence of folklore: traditional, expressive behavior generated by people as they interact with one another.

Not all symbolism is folklore. The company pin or T-shirt with its logo is a manufactured rather than a handmade item, and it is a product of the formal organization rather than informal interaction. The company-sponsored sales meeting, the official awards banquet and pep rally, the personnel department's reward system, the administration's allocation of resources— although symbolic—are not generated out of organization members' face-to-face interaction and communication. As one employee remarked about "official" ceremonies and celebrations, "They seem too much like work." Folklore arises more spontaneously as an expression of people's feelings and ideas in specific circumstances.

Distinctions between institutional symbols and folklore assume importance in studies of organizational symbolism in regard to documentation, analysis, and intervention. Are these managerial symbols, created as a means of control, or are they examples of symbolic behavior generated spontaneously by organization members as a way of making sense of situations, expressing feelings, coping with vicissitudes, or even opposing management? Discovering that narrating influences informal learning of values or that spontaneous festive events express social support does not mean that purposefully creating or promoting certain organizational stories and instituting celebrative occasions will have the same effects (Vance, 1991).

For those interested in symbolism and everyday life in an organization, folklore becomes a valuable source of information and object of study (Jones, 1990, 1991b, 1991c). In an essay on organizational folklore, Yiannis Gabriel (1991, p. 871) writes that traditional narratives present a reality in organizational life often inaccessible through conventional sources and techniques of data gathering: "People may be able to articulate their experiences in and around organizations in deeper and more accurate ways through stories, jokes, and other symbols than through straight talk." One reason is that symbolic behavior, in the form of oft-told jokes and tales, "permits the expression of meaning by surrounding it in a smoke screen of poetic license which enables it to evade various social and mental censors"

(p. 871). In addition, the presence or absence of food sharing among organization members, the way they greet or refer to one another, what they celebrate, the kinds of photocopier lore they display, etc. embody feelings about themselves and an organization. Various examples of folklore may challenge, convey, or reinforce values; help make sense of events; entertain and provide intellectual and sensory stimuli; subvert the system; contribute to bonding and the creation of community. The upshot is that everyday life in organizations involves a great deal of symbolic communication and interaction. In turn, much of this expressive behavior is or becomes traditional, exhibiting continuities through time and consistencies in space; it has "historical halos" (Denzin, 1983, p. 134) as well as cultural ones.

Although many conceptions of "culture" have been advanced, most hark back to early usage in folklore studies and anthropology as eventually articulated by the anthropological folklorist E. B. Tylor (1871/1958, p. 1): "Culture, or Civilization, taken in its wide ethnographic sense, is that complex whole which includes knowledge, belief, art, morals, laws, customs, and any other capabilities and habits acquired by man as a member of society."

According to this definition, culture consists of assumptions ("beliefs") and values ("morals," "laws") along with their manifestations ("art," "customs," "habits"). By contending that these are acquired by people as members of a group, Tylor sought to differentiate idiosyncratic beliefs and behaviors from socially constructed and transmitted ones and to distinguish actions based on instinct from behavior that is learned from other human beings. Scholars before and after Tylor have tried to identify the various elements and their relationship within the "complex whole" called culture (Kroeber & Kluckhohn, 1952).

Notions of culture in the organizational literature vary. To some, culture is simply "how things are done around here" (Deal & Kennedy, 1982, p. 4). Others consider it "shared values" (Peters & Waterman, 1982) or a symbolic system of shared meanings (Smircich, 1983b). Yet others conceive of it as customs on one hand and values on the other (Louis, 1983). A popular conception was proposed by Schein (1985, pp. 5-21), namely, that culture is "a learned product of group experience" consisting of "a pattern of basic assumptions" about how to think and feel in regard to "problems of external adaptation and internal integration." He places the various "elements" of culture in a hierarchy. At the basic level are assumptions about the environment, human nature and relationships that are taken for granted. These relate to values that matter most in an organization. Both assumptions and values are expressed through "artifacts" (technology, art, and visible behavior patterns).

Schein's conception has been challenged on several grounds, from its reification of symbolic behavior as objects or entities ("artifacts") to its being a static rather than a dynamic model of relationships between elements of culture (Hatch, 1993a). Some argue that although symbols may embody assumptions and values, symbolic behavior such as storytelling, or ritualized interactions can just as readily create beliefs and construct realities for organizational participants as express already existing ones. Others contend that the culture construct itself is a "symbol" (Spradley, 1979), even a "root metaphor" in organizational analysis (Smircich, 1983a, 1985; Smircich & Calás, 1987).

Clearly, the three concepts of symbolism, folklore, and culture are interrelated. Some symbols correlate with assumptions and values of a group and its culture. Most symbolic behaviors are examples of folklore, because much of social life involves interaction and communication during the course of which social routines develop, stories are told repeatedly, familiar expressions are used, rituals are enacted, joking and kidding are engaged in, and customs are perpetuated; these often serve as a basis for inferring a group's culture.

In the final analysis, writes Linda Smircich (1985, p. 65), organizations are "symbolically constituted worlds" and "symbolic forms." As "representations of our humanity," such as art and music, organizations "can be known through acts of appreciation." As symbolic creations, such as novels or poems, "they can be known through acts of critical reading and interpretation." As symbolic forms, such as religion and folklore, "they are displays of the meaning of life" (see Strati, 1992; Turner, 1990b, 1992).

Functionalism and Symbolic Interpretivism

Two major approaches to studying organizational symbolism are sociocultural functionalism and symbolic interpretivism. In 1935, social anthropologist Radcliffe-Brown pointed out that the concept of function in social science is based on an analogy between social life and organic life. In human society, individuals are connected by social relations into an integrated whole like a living organism. The function of any recurrent social activity is its contribution to maintaining structural continuity, just as the parts ("life processes") of an organism function together to maintain the life of the organism (Radcliffe-Brown, 1935). Later, in summarizing some of the research on folklore, cultural anthropologist Bascom (1954) concluded that traditional symbolic forms validate culture, educate members of a group about values and behavioral norms, and ensure conformity by applying social pressure and exerting social control; all this adds up to a single function—that of preserving the stability of culture.

Sociocultural functionalism, then, entails an integration theory (Burrell & Morgan, 1979): Society and culture are relatively homogeneous and stable, and they consist of interrelated, integrated elements, each functioning to perpetuate the structure. Hence, functionalism tends toward determinism; people's behavior is conditioned by external circumstances. Ontologically, functionalism is objectivist in assuming the reality to be studied is external to the individual. Epistemologically it is positivist (or "realist"), contending that knowledge is hard, real, and capable of being conveyed as causal relationships or general laws. Methodologically the perspective is nomothetic, testing a priori hypotheses by using quantitative methods to produce law-like statements. Description in research reports tends to be "thin": summaries, paraphrasings, reconstructions, and parenthetical references rather than detailed accounts of symbolic behavior or extensive quoting of informants. Writers typically refer to systems, functions, and survival. Often they adopt a social engineering philosophy, proposing ways in which artifacts and their sociocultural functions can be identified and the symbols put to use.

Many who advocate symbolic interpretivism write about, in the words of Barry Turner (1990b, pp. 85, 88, 89), "the sensuous aspects of lived experience," "the affective and the aesthetic," and the organizational world as a "sensual and emotional realm, replete with its own ceremonies, rites and dramas"; they contend that they are less concerned with instrumentality "than with understanding, with meaning, with interpretation" (see also Alvesson & Berg, 1992; Schultz, 1994; Smircich & Calás, 1987). The approach is subjectivist, viewing reality as the product of individual consciousness, creativity, and construction (Strati, 1995; Turner, 1992). Methodologically, symbolic interpretivism seeks firsthand knowledge, "lived" concepts, and meanings and intentions through the researcher's involvement in the everyday flow of life. Research is iterative, with understanding of social action developing as themes unfold in the setting (Smircich, 1983b, p. 167). Documentation and presentation entail "thick" description of social interaction and personal expression to capture and convey behavior, intentions, and inferences based on the assumption that "every human situation is novel, emergent, and filled with multiple, often conflicting, meanings and interpretations" (Denzin, 1983, p. 133).

Symbolic interpretivists' reliance on "empathy and involvement and the use of the self as an instrument of research" (Smircich, 1983b, p. 171) may raise questions about validity and reliability. Those who employ qualitative methods on behalf of symbolic interpretivism verify concepts, meanings, and interpretations by collecting multiple forms of evidence and using a variety of techniques (observing as well as interviewing, asking different people about the same topic, querying the same person on different occasions), acknowledging disagreements in subjects' interpretations and seeking reasons for them, using the concept with the subjects during research to determine if one really has gained access to the insiders' world of meaning and action, and taking the data and interpretations back to those studied for assessment, correction, confirmation, or alternative theories. Reliability—the presentation of dependable and trustworthy findings—depends on these verification procedures, combined with full disclosure of how information was collected, making visible the process of interpretation, supporting theoretical claims with evidence from informants' accounts, considering alternative explanations and theories, and making primary data available to other researchers (Jorgensen, 1989, pp. 36-38; Riessman, 1993, pp. 64-68). Evaluation rests on the integrity, soundness, believability, and persuasiveness of the analysis and on its enlargement of our understanding of individual behavior and of social life (Denzin, 1983, 1989; Riessman, 1993; Smircich, 1983b).

Why Study Symbolism in Organizations?

"Symbolic aspects of organizations are worth exploring," writes Barry Turner (1992, p. 63), "to understand the aesthetic and stylistic identities which are generated within them, to increase our knowledge of how boundaries are constituted around organizational identities and to promote strategic change." In other words, studying symbolism is one means of achieving a fuller understanding of the behavior in and of organizations; it offers opportunities to apply hypotheses to solve practical problems faced by organizations and their members.

Some researchers, for instance, propose studying symbolism to gain an inside look at organizing under conditions of uncertainty (Hatch, 1983b), comprehend how ideological contradictions are mediated or mitigated by "myths" (Scheid-Cook, 1988), and appreciate paradox and ambiguity expressed in dress, stories, office decor (Meyerson, 1990), or irony (Hatch & Ehrlich, 1993). Others orient research toward ways of transforming organizations, intervening in organizational processes, and/or affecting organizational outcomes through the purposeful use of metaphors (Barrett & Cooperrider, 1990; Sackmann, 1989; Westley, 1990), stories and story-telling (Boje, 1991a; Vance, 1991; Wilkins & Thompson, 1991), and rituals and ceremonials (Beyer & Trice, 1988; Harris & Sutton, 1986).

Sociocultural functionalism seems more inclined to recommend application (Czarniawska-Joerges, 1992, pp. 166-171). After all, the perspective focuses on the function of artifacts and activities for maintaining structural continuity. It is a relatively easy step from positing general meanings of a symbol within a social system to proposing ways of using, say, stories to convey organizational philosophy, creating transitional mechanisms such as parting rituals to influence reorganization, and substituting metaphors in attempts to change organizational culture.

Application within a symbolic interpretivist perspective (when considered at all) is more broadly self-reflective because research tends to focus on multiple and multilayered meanings, even conflicting interpretations, of symbolic behavior in situated events (the immediate contexts of performance). In the words of Linda Smircich (1983b, p. 164),

> The researcher reflects back to a group a many-sided image of the systems of meaning in use. Through the process of guided self-reflection, a deeper understanding of the dynamics of behavior can be gained. The increased awareness may spark insights that lead to change.

Although most research on organizational symbolism concerns institutions and culture and dwells on "social" constructions and "shared" meanings or values, the behavior of individuals and the uniqueness of events are essential considerations. Depending on circumstances, symbolic behavior such as gossip and rumors may produce anxiety for some people, kidding and joking can relieve tensions and stress, stories might project frustrations into "fictive playgrounds," and rites of passage may ease emotional transitions; in other words, the symbolization is correlated with psychological states and processes. Further, individuals develop repertoires of organizational or occupational jargon, traditional expressions, folk beliefs, and "local knowledge"; they then use these aspects of culture as a personal resource, transforming socially constructed symbols to make them compatible with their own experiences, biases, and preferences. Finally, just as each person uses familiar symbols uniquely, so is each instance of symbolic behavior situationally idiosyncratic, with the purpose, setting, and number and nature of people involved all determining what form an example of symbolic behavior takes and what its meanings are (Georges & Jones, 1995).

2. GETTING STARTED

Studying the symbolic in organizations involves such questions as where to look for meanings, how to document behavior and settings, and how to interpret what one finds. The approach taken here advocates observing behaviors that enact and produce meanings (i.e., dynamic acts of symbolizing) rather than the mere collection of "symbols" and "artifacts" (onto which researchers all too often impose meaning). It recommends focusing on specific circumstances and situated events. And it proposes the appreciation of symbolic behavior as "performance."

Attribute it to "cultural lag," perhaps (MacIver, 1942, p. 280), but the rush to use organizational culture or symbolism to explain and manage social systems outpaced the development of methods to document it. Much research on culture in the 1980s was quantitative. It relied on questionnaires and survey instruments that obviously could not witness events or produce rich descriptions of the behaviors in which values and assumptions are embedded or through which participants construct the organization and their understanding of it (a few investigators did try to augment quantitative methods with some qualitative techniques, e.g., Duncan, 1989; Siehl & Martin, 1988).

Qualitative methods appear better suited to a symbolic interpretive approach (sometimes using surveys as an adjunct but not as the primary tool). Through observation, participant observation, and interviewing in depth, the researcher attempts to gain an *emic* or insider's view of organizational life, experiencing as directly as possible the situations in which members are immersed. Understanding evolves as people talk about their experiences and perceptions and as the researcher takes part in them (Jones, 1988; Schwartzman, 1993; Spradley, 1979, 1980; Van Maanen, 1982, 1988). Although techniques might need modification, the overall methods of qualitative research fit well with the current focus on the expressive, sensuous, aesthetic, emotional, stylistic, and performative aspects of organizations (Turner, 1990a, p. 3).

Many of the examples of techniques that I discuss are drawn from personal experience, appear in the writings of folklorists, or derive from the work of researchers (largely European) associated with SCOS (Standing Committee on Organizational Symbolism). This choice reflects my bias as a folklorist but also the fact that although some essays on symbolism have appeared in leading U.S. management and administrative science journals, much of symbolic interpretive research occurs in other fields and finds voice in other venues. Symbolic interpretivism is interdisciplinary, international, and relatively new to many involved in organization studies. The remainder of this volume describes techniques for identifying, documenting, and presenting symbols and symbolic behavior largely from an interpretive approach that emphasizes symbolism as behavior and performance.

Seeking Star Performers and Key Informants

Everyone tells stories, that is, describes things that have happened. We often illustrate a point by narrating, or we narrate about something first and then inferences are drawn and discussed from the example we present. In addition, everyone celebrates, ritualizes, plays, and uses figurative language. We all make things, even if it is only arranging files, tidying up the office, or surrounding our work area with memorabilia. We also reflect on issues and offer interpretations and advice. Some people spend more time doing one or another of these things, or they are said to do them more skillfully. These are the experts, "wise" women and men, and performers: the "active tradition bearers" (von Sydow, 1948, pp. 52, 55).

In any recurrent social situation, a few individuals are particularly knowledgeable and articulate (i.e., they make better "informants"; Sanday, 1983, p. 21). Certain people are recognized as "storytellers," others are noted for peppering their speech with numerous sayings or are masters of jargon, and yet others are adept at organizing and directing social events (meetings, ceremonies, etc.). This fact does not justify observing and interviewing only a few individuals to the exclusion of all others; rather, it directs attention to the areas of expertise that different people have and guides in identifying those symbolic, performative genres that an individual finds congenial and frequently uses in communication and interaction. Discovering who is the expert about a particular matter, who performs well in which symbolic modes (and what their "repertoires" are; see Georges, 1994), and what are the pervading symbolic forms and themes is an essential step toward understanding the construction and interpretation of meaning, because these people are doing much of the constructing and interpreting.

One way to find such performers and experts is to observe; another way is to ask. Whether inquiry is discreet or takes the form of public announcement depends on circumstances. Lars Edgren (1990), who led a short-term "culture diagnosis" project solicited by a Scandinavian service company, had arrangements made in advance:

> Our client had already informed the managers about our visit, and they had found a contact person at each unit for us. Every general manager had further prepared for our visit by ensuring that employees would be willing to be interviewed during the day. (p. 184)

How one finds an expert or a particular kind of performer among the assembled employees, however, entails more specific inquiry. Jack Santino's (1978a, 1978b) account of his research on narratives in the communications and transportation industries provides an example of one way to start identifying performers and uncovering themes in performances.

When Santino worked at the Smithsonian Institution's annual summer American Folklife Festival on the Mall, he met Roger Culler, a cable splicer for the telephone company who demonstrated his skills as a "working American" (one of the emphases of the festival):

> Roger appreciated the attention of having people sit down and talk to him about his job, his skills, and his life, and he recognized the possibilities inherent in any project that encourages workers to tell their stories and speak their mind. (Santino, 1978b, p. 37)

Culler invited Santino to do research on himself and his coworkers. Santino attended a monthly meeting of the Central Office Club, hoping to elicit some narratives.

The president called the meeting to order. After the group discussed the first point of business, Santino was introduced as a guest from the Smithsonian Institution. "Why don't we just let him come up here and let him tell us what it is he wants?" said the president to the assembled crowd.

Santino writes,

> Standing there alone. All eyes on me. . . . One of the hardest things in the world to do is to explain to people the kind of story I am interested in, or even to explain what is meant by a "story." I described the festival briefly, emphasizing the fact that through the Communications Workers of America, their union, phone company workers had been represented at it, and that Roger Culler—one of *them*—had participated. They listened. I was hoping to God I was making sense.
>
> As generally as I could, I described stories about guys on the job, characters, guys they maybe worked with, guys they maybe only heard about. Clowns. People who are very, very good at what they do. Whatever, I wanted to hear stories about the job.
>
> "In other words, you want all the bullshit," somebody yelled (pp. 39-48).

Santino responded affirmatively. Then they returned to their meeting, took care of other business, and began eating. Santino was reluctant to interrupt them but Culler urged him to start asking for stories. As Santino began walking toward the back of the auditorium in search of likely prospects to interview, one person called out to him, " 'Hey! What kind of stories are you after? Well, is this the kind of thing you mean?' " This person described what happened one time to a fellow named Dave Barnes, exactly what Santino had in mind.

"Yeah, hold on a minute, let me get my tape recorder," said Santino.

"Dave Barnes . . . he was out installing phones in a lady's house and a little dog was barking around at his feet, so he was all worried about it, and the lady said, 'Don't worry about it, she's been spayed.' And he just told her, 'I'm not worried about the dog screwing me, I'm worried about her biting me!' And that's the way he is."

Speaking was Jerry Hood, an excellent storyteller. Ed Follier was at the table, telling a lot of stories, mostly on himself. Dick Kaiser, a young man who has been with the company for eight years, divided his attention between my microphone and his card game, while Dick Smith, who was sitting at the other end of the long table, occasionally contributed a story and an idea (pp. 39-48).

Santino recorded other stories that night. Some involved people who were with the company long ago; others described events concerning present employees (including some at the interview). Stories centered on the antics of "characters," relationships between subordinates and supervisors ("bosses"), accidents, and the kinds of situations or interpersonal problems typically encountered when doing one's job.

Before long, Santino, who had begun as "a pilgrim and a stranger," realized a number of things. The technique of a group interview dwelling on a particular topic (a *focus group*) can be extremely effective in eliciting information, attitudes, and perceptions—especially when people are asked simply to tell stories about work and fellow employees' experiences: One story triggers another and then another (*serial stories*). Narrators revealed to Santino their views of the organization and how it had changed over time (in regard to management philosophy and procedures), and they expressed their feelings about particular supervisors and some types of customers.

Looking over his transcript of tape-recorded stories from that night, Santino discovered recurrent themes. Some stories described the first day on the job. Others expressed the hostility toward authority . . .; the feeling that the old days were somehow better days, in that there was a greater tolerance of individuality; and the cautionary tale of the worker who was in a hurry, was negligent, and got hurt as a result. (1978b, p. 53)

Some tales involved characters ranging from daredevils to tricksters to heroes battling bureaucratic restraints and infringements, feeling resentful at their subordinate status, subverting the system, or reversing status relationships. Through additional research, guided by specific questions and hypotheses generated from his early explorations, Santino discovered ambiguities in service roles, reasons for ambivalent feelings of people in these roles, and ways in which individuals attempt to cope with stress in the organizational workplace.

For Santino, getting started in his research that first night and finding performers

turned out to be no problem at all. Not only did men come to me while I was at Jerry's table, in one case a man came over and pointed someone out to me and said, "Listen. You have to talk to that guy over there. He won't come to you." So I made it a point to get over to him. In fact, there was so much interest shown by so many men that I had to leave Jerry's table after a fairly lengthy stay. (1978b, pp. 53-54)

Identifying Performance Settings and Events

At the monthly meeting of the Central Office Club where Santino sought narrators, men were playing cards, talking, and telling stories. This was a "natural setting" for such behavior. If there was anything "artificial" about the situation, it was that Santino called attention to stories and storytelling as a subject worthy of research. In seeking narrators who were recognized for their skills and performances and to whom others deferred, Santino wished to identify the individuals who took an active role in the "social construction of reality" through this kind of symbolic behavior and to record some examples. By being present as a researcher and asking for stories, Santino may have "led" others to perform in this role to a greater extent than they otherwise would have, or even to tell particular stories (his introductory reference to the kinds of stories he sought and his positive response to proffered examples sent signals to others). But this was only one setting, and Santino merely was attempting to get started.

For decades researchers have employed such concepts as *work group* and *subculture* to delineate segments of organizations for observation and analysis. The fact that work is carried on within a specific location, often a bounded area, contributes to the focus on work settings and groups in them as isolable units with distinct cultures (Applebaum, 1981, 1987). Custom, play, artistic production, and aesthetic response are certainly inherent in the work process (Dandridge, 1988; Dewhurst, 1988; Garson, 1975; Jones, 1984, 1987, 1991c; Lockwood, 1984; Roy, 1959-1960). The place of work and the process of working, therefore, are obviously appropriate situations in which to observe symbolic behavior. Santino, however, began his research not in the workplace but at a social club. Hence, other locales and more specific circumstances within or outside the work setting are sites of symbolic performances.

In her study of a community mental health center, Helen Schwartzman (1989, 1993, pp. 38-46) focused on meetings (usually ignored in research as too commonplace and routine), conceiving of them as significant "communication events" and "a constitutive social form." Schwartzman (1993, pp. 39-40) writes, "In my view it is important to emphasize that individuals do not and cannot act outside of forms such as communication events like meetings, which are used to generate interaction as well as to interpret what it means." It is through meetings (and the storytelling and use of metaphors in them) that individuals

make sense of or "see" the organization and their actions in it. . . . Staff and board members saw their world as a battleground and they became caught up in a battle for control, while at the same time viewing one another's activities as "out of control."

Debra Meyerson also observed meetings, both formal and informal, and interviewed people in work settings when she conducted research on hospital social workers. She soon realized that social workers experience feelings of ambiguity in their role (their occupation includes a number of tasks that can be performed by others, and many social workers hold contradictory beliefs about the medical model that is the dominant ideology of health care). Ambiguity involves such emotions as confusion, ambivalence, and cynicism; as "undesirable" feelings and signs of "weakness" in a medical center, they are rarely expressed in formal settings. Thus, "it was during loosely structured meetings, elevator rides to and from meetings, chats in the hall, parties, and workshop breaks that confusion among hospital social workers came to light" in joking remarks, stories, metaphors, and traditional expressions (Meyerson, 1990, p. 299). Ambivalence could be seen in appearance. "One social worker usually dressed 'funky social work,' but on a particular day looked, as the supervisor pointed out, 'really professional' " (p. 301). Meyerson also noticed office decor. "For example, one social worker's office appeared strikingly void of social work books, journals, or memorabilia" (p. 301). Instead, magazines and novels filled bookshelves while comic images and personal photos adorned the walls. "The occupant had a personal stereo on one shelf and a stockpile of food on another. Yet a framed diploma was displayed prominently above her desk," the incongruity of it all expressing her ambivalence about professionalism (p. 301). Sites of symbolic performances that Meyerson observed closely, then, were personally decorated offices, elevator rides, the hallway, and other nonwork, between-work, or break-in-work situations.

Work breaks themselves are symbolic forms and the theater for performances (Stanley, 1977). "Choir practice" is a familiar example, brought to public attention by such fictionalized accounts as Joseph Wambaugh's *The Choirboys* (1975) and the 1977 film based on it. Phylliss Henry, experienced as a police officer herself, included choir practice in her study of the contexts in which "war stories" are told. Also known as "having a beer," "bull session," "story hour," "a coffee klatch," and "beer with the gang," the term *choir practice* "refers to a segment of time (generally, but not always, after work) when a group of officers get together, and the activities [talking, joking, storytelling, drinking, prankish behavior] that take place during that time period" (Henry, 1988, p. 141). Being invited to participate may symbolize social acceptance as well as trust (that others will not reveal rule violations described in stories or disclose expressions of confusion, ambivalence, fear, anger, etc.)—at least for younger, white, male police officers. Choir practice and symbolic activities within it can convey information, make sense of events, provide social support, express "controlled" or inhibited emotions, and affirm a sense of professional self-worth for some police officers (Henry, 1988, pp. 159, 162-176).

Symbolic Domains as Interpretive Frameworks for Performance

As the examples above illustrate, a social club, elevator ride, hallway encounter, personally decorated office, or work break may be a site of symbolic expression and interaction. The same space might host different expressive behaviors—for example, when a room serves as the location of ritual staff meetings but is also a place for informal parties and festive events. In this instance, performances that differ dramatically occur in the same location; chairs and table might be reconfigured or decoration added to signal a change in how the space should be interpreted and therefore what behaviors are appropriate. The events have the character of "symbolic domains" and thus alter conceptions of and activities within the setting. Based on research by Goffman (1959) and Spradley (1979), Majken Schultz (1991, pp. 489, 491) writes of symbolic domain as a "distinct set of social definitions and meanings." Rather than a particular place or time, it is a "bounded interpretative framework." Different work settings or other sites may invoke a single symbolic domain, and several symbolic domains can characterize a single site.

Schultz applies the concept to the activities of 10 managers (6 men, 4 women) in a departmental organization within a Danish ministry. She focuses on one work group, the managers, and their subculture. There are two work locales—the managers' offices and the room where meetings are presided over by the Minister. There is also the hallway leading from individual offices to the meeting room. The concept of symbolic domain helps uncover a wealth of behavior in these circumstances, particularly with respect to how managers switch back and forth among interpretive frameworks, encode the transitions, and interpret one another's talk and action.

A headline in the morning paper, a note from the Minister indicating the possibility of future talks, rumors, or even a knock on the door: Any of these events can trigger a reframing of space and activity from "mundane monastery" to "fire station" and transform the speed and style of a manager's behavior. Managers quickly rise and leave meetings, rushing down the corridors "sometimes with papers flapping." Gestures, facial expressions, and tone become serious (as in the statement, "The Minister wants to see me right away; it can't wait"). Immediately on hearing that the Minister has decided not to raise a certain issue, managers slow down, hang around the corridors, and talk with colleagues for a while. "All managers draw upon the same repertoire of ritualized movements, gestures and statements" (Schultz, 1991, p. 500).

Many changes in behavior characterize and signal a shift to the symbolic domain of the weekly "meeting with the sage":

> Paper is the dominant symbol of both ordinary managerial activity and day-to-day talks with the Minister. Files, notes, speeches, reports, summaries, memorandums, letters are piling up on most managers' desks as symbols of the hard effort and endless routines of the mundane monastery. The most precious symbol of the fire station is the little blue slip from the Minister, creating excitement and a disturbance. (p. 501)

But managers go to the weekly meeting empty-handed; they have left the dominant symbols of life "outside." As the Minister and her secretary make their entrance through large double doors, the managers become silent, lean stiffly against their wooden chairs, and assume nearly identical facial expressions. Behaving similarly, they become equally close—symbolically—to the core of political power and convey, again symbolically, their deference and obedience to the Minister. After she leaves, the managers gradually begin to raise their voices and take on different, more individualistic expressions. Some hang around a few minutes, then retreat to their desks to ponder what the meeting might mean to their future activities; others rush to their offices, expecting to be called by the Minister because small winks and nods at the meeting portend urgent matters.

The managers work within different symbolic domains, each with a distinct way of framing and interpreting talk and action and defining roles and behavior within a particular setting. The managers keep all the domains in mind, switching back and forth among them as circumstances change. Because the same phenomenon occurs in various organizations, the notion of symbolic domain can help guide observations in research on the social construction of organization, indicating where to look and why.

3. OBSERVING PERFORMANCES, STYLISTICS, AND MEANING MAKING

Observation is a cornerstone of qualitative studies. It is frequently mentioned as essential to *triangulation* (the name refers to the navigational procedure of using multiple reference points to establish location), which combines several techniques of data gathering to corroborate information (Jick, 1983; Patton, 1990, p. 187). As such, it is deemed one of the important "checks and controls" in fieldwork (Goldstein, 1964; Jackson, 1987; Jorgensen, 1989; Kaplan, 1964; Spradley, 1980; Whyte, 1984).

Why Observe, and What?

One oft-cited reason for observing is to substantiate what people say. Advocating triangulation, W. Jack Duncan (1989, pp. 232-233) and a team of graduate students used observation to check information obtained through interviews and questionnaires in their research on a hospital rehabilitation center. Observation of the center's state-of-the-art equipment, employees' casual dress, and the prevalence of positive rituals and ceremonies confirmed that, as respondents had contended, the center was a favored child of the funding agency, hierarchy was minimized, and the unit's success owed much to social routines characterized by congeniality and social support.

Sometimes observation reveals inconsistencies or contradictions:

> Consider the recurring statements I heard from many officers attesting to the "fact" that they felt under no pressure whatsoever to make certain kinds of arrests when on patrol. Their actions often belied their words for, on many occasions, I sat with these same officers in their prowl cars outside dimly lit taverns simply waiting for the first unsteady (and unlucky) patron to drive away. . . . [The arrests] were said by the men to be necessary for "getting the drunk-hunting sergeant off our backs for awhile." (Van Maanen, 1983, p. 45)

This example shows several things. When people lie, Van Maanen notes, it is probably about things that matter most to them. Filled with meaning, the seeming falsehood is a symbolic construction. In this instance, "It was of some importance apparently to these patrolmen that they be seen as autonomous, independent actors in the police drama for they took great care to present themselves in such a manner" (p. 45). For other researchers, the discrepancy in data might have constituted a verification issue, raising questions about what is true; for Van Maanen, it is an example of meaning making through symbolic expression.

Van Maanen witnessed the contradiction between words and actions not simply through observation, but *participant* observation (Kluckhohn, 1940); he was a researcher who also functioned in a role typical within the group studied, and he took part in the same activities. He went through 13 weeks of training as a police academy recruit. "I made no effort to conceal my identity [as researcher] or general purposes behind my work," he writes (1982, p. 112; on overt versus covert observation, see Lofland, 1971, p. 93; Nickerson, 1983, p. 122; Schwartzman, 1993, pp. 52-53).

> Following graduation, I moved to the street and assumed a less participative [and more research-oriented] role though, on my body, I still carried a badge and gun. These symbols of membership signified to others my more or less public commitment to share the risks of the police life. (p. 113)

By being a participant observer, Van Maanen was privy to behaviors in a wide range of symbolic domains seldom glimpsed by outsiders, such as roll call, stakeouts, arrests, cruising, choir practice, coffee breaks, the locker room, and so on.

In sum, one reason for observing is to validate data, confirming statements or uncovering differences between what is professed and practiced. Another is to discover that which people do not see, say, or know. Observation can bring to light what is taken for granted or out of awareness and give form to matters that people find difficult to verbalize or cannot describe in sufficient detail. Through observation, researchers can see technical processes at work or witness a drama unfold, and therefore they need not depend on someone else's verbal description. Third, observing enables one to sense more directly and immediately, especially by participating in the event oneself, what insiders experience and feel; therefore, it helps the researcher understand how others make meanings and what some of these meanings are (see, e.g., Smircich, 1983b, p. 168). It is, then, a way of knowing, one that is largely sensuous and even aesthetic. This renders it especially appropriate to studying symbolism, which involves feelings and the senses.

Below is a list of matters to observe in regard to symbolic performances, including the immediate physical and social settings that situate the behavior, style, and aesthetics of performance (the list is adapted from Goldstein, 1964, pp. 91-93; Schwartzman, 1993). In keeping with a symbolic interpretive approach, the list assumes the need for "thick" description that probes people's intentions, meanings, and inferences (Denzin, 1983, pp. 143-145) as well as the networks of social relationships and "webs of significance" that people weave (Geertz, 1973).

The Physical Setting

Indoors: The location within the building, the size and shape of room used, its condition, distance from or proximity to other rooms, its normal use, adornments of the room or lack of these (pictures, furniture, award plaques), lighting (including windows and natural light), and even temperature, unusual sounds or noises, and unusual odors

Outdoors: Location, scenic layout, weather conditions, temperature, sounds, smells

The Social Setting

For persons present: Number, sex, age, names, status in community or organization, role and status in the symbolic domain (i.e., as the narrator of a story, organizer of a ritual, honoree in the ceremony, or a noted proverb user, joke teller, or initiator of social events), relationship of individuals to one another, placement or position in the physical setting, general appearance and dress; also, the occasion for the performance, the manner in which participants were brought together, and the availability of food or drink (and their source—e.g., it may mean one thing at a birthday party for participants to make food at home to bring but may be something entirely different if the foods are simply purchased)

Interaction Among Participants

Initiator of action, special roles in interaction, personal incentives, methods of encouragement or disapproval (gestures, sounds, facial expressions, comments), competing actions (interruptions, conversation while performance is taking place, separate performances going on at the same time), rapport or empathy actions, or joining in with performers

Performance

Framing: Introductory commentary (in storytelling, ritual, ceremony, meetings), closing commentary, presentation and use of special equipment or objects (e.g., arriving at meeting with calendar and notebook), other metacommunication devices to signal the interpretive context

Genres: Dominant symbolic form (ceremony, meeting, narrating) and subordinate forms (particular mode of dress, use of traditional expressions and metaphors, joking, special objects, etc.)

Channels of Communication/Coding: Speaking, note taking, communication via computer, memos, physical motion, gestures, facial expressions, use of objects

Styles: Characteristic manner and stylistics of performance—for example, a speaker's posture, attitude, intonation, voice rhythm, speaking rate, pitch, vocal intensity, facial expressions, gestures, voice imitation of characters, repetition, interjections, pauses, and digressions—or an object maker's choice of materials, themes, images, placement of elements within the whole

Aesthetics and Interpretations: Sentiments expressed, including statements of approval or disapproval, comments on quality of performance, emotional displays (laughing, crying, anger, etc.), bodily expressiveness (e.g., open, expansive gestures vs. closed, "protective" or defensive ones); the intensity of emotions; verbal or nonverbal responses that suggest interpretation (nodding, evidence of disagreement, changes in behavior during and after performance)

Performance Norms: Standards for appropriate behavior and deviations from normal performance (based on observer's prior experiences with performer or on comments from other observers)

Time and Duration

Time of day when symbolic performance begins and ends; time devoted to introductions, performance, intermissions, and socializing; duration of individual performances (whether a story, ritual, or use of a proverb or example of jargon/argot); exact order in which performative acts occur; time and duration of unusual occurrences (e.g., interruptions)

The Observer

Observer's own role in context, the position of observer, the observer's state of mind and physical condition, factors contributing to observer's comfort or discomfort, events affecting the observer

This list is suggestive, not exhaustive. Some matters might seem of limited importance in one situation, critical in another (see Chapter 5). By directing attention at the physical and social settings, participants' interactions, the sentiments expressed, and even the observer, the list indicates that expressive behavior is not simply disembodied symbols. Performances are enacted, situated events. When people communicate and interact symbolically, what they express and how they do so are affected by the specifics of time, place, and experience. Creation and meanings depend on who is present (including the researcher; see Georges & Jones, 1980; Van Maanen, 1988), what their roles and relationships are, how they conceive of one another, and whatever else is going on at the time (Georges, 1979, 1981, 1987, 1990).

Examples discussed earlier illustrate researchers' attention to some of the categories in the list above. Schultz noted the time and duration of symbolic behavior of managers in the Danish ministry, Duncan's team dwelt on the physical and social settings of symbolic acts in a rehab center, and Van Maanen focused on the performances and sentiments of police officers. All three paid attention to activities and verbal expressions, less to objects (although Schultz observed the presence or absence of paper, and Duncan's team noticed the center's modern equipment and freshly painted surroundings). The tangible aspects of organization are the most visible and yet also the most problematic methodologically because they do not talk or act.

Viewing Material Behavior as Stylized Performance

Typically, objects are treated as a backdrop, part of the physical setting for other performances (some exceptions are Strati, 1992; Witkin, 1990a; Yanow, 1994). Sometimes an object is placed center stage "as a thing in itself, with its own significance incarnated within its own existence" (Armstrong, 1971, p. xvi). Either way, few categories of observational data are noted. If objects are viewed as *material behavior* (Jones, in press), however, they can be seen as symbolic performances that, like other displays of meaning, occur in various social and physical settings and involve roles and interactions. A largely overlooked genre, the personal decoration of work areas illustrates how objects may be conceived of as material behavior, that is, the tangible aspects or manifestations of individuals' experiences, sentiments, and meaning making.

Several years ago I observed an office occupied by three teaching assistants. All decorated their work area with mementos, photos, and posters, and two displayed work-related memos, policy statements, and deadlines. One teaching assistant taped job-related information on the wall directly in front of her at eye level, as though she had to focus on what she must do. To her left on the side of a filing cabinet she exhibited an example of photocopier lore—a cartoon of a menacing grouch, below which a caption warns others not to speak until he has had his morning's coffee. A student entering the office and looking at the teaching assistant at her desk would see both the instructor and the grouch. On the wall immediately to the right of the teaching assistant's desk was another example of photocopier lore in the form of an "Answers Price List," from "Answers" for 75 cents to "Answers (requiring thought)" for $1.25 to "Answers (correct)" for $2.50 but with the notation that "Dumb Looks Are Still Free." Although a seated student blocked it from view, the teaching assistant would always know the item was there; certainly she saw it before a student sat down and after leaving. Higher up the wall she taped a poster depicting a knight slaying a dragon. To look at the image when seated, she would have to lean back in her chair, head tilted, eyes up—behavior associated with reverie. Not surprisingly, the course for which she was a teaching assistant was a far cry from her specialty in medieval literature. In addition, she was introverted, uncomfortable in the classroom, and impatient with students.

The decoration of another teaching assistant's work area in the same room can best be described as dense and richly textured. Mementos and memorabilia cascaded down the wall, splashing onto the top of her desk (work-related information was on the wall to her right, visible only peripherally). They included colorful postcards of places she had visited, a handmade greeting card from someone who had occupied the office the year before, a framed photo of her brother and his wife who were in graduate school elsewhere and whom she missed, and many other items, including objects on her desk that could be held and moved around. Often topics of conversation, these things also were touchstones when the teaching assistant's self-assurance faltered (Bronner, 1986, pp. 5-12; Kirshenblatt-Gimblett, 1989; Musello, 1992).

The third teaching assistant had a row of neatly arranged books on her desk that she used for reference and course preparation. On the wall in front of her was a poster-size color photo of Munich, a city she had never been to but planned to visit in a few months after earning her graduate degree.

That the teaching assistants decorated their work areas at all, let alone with mementos, souvenirs, benchmark objects, and tokens of concern, indicates much about human psychology and has implications for organizational behavior research, office design, and managing organizations (Doxtater, 1990; Hatch & Jones, 1994; Steele, 1973). Sociologically, the extent to which people's personalization of space "mesh" with one another may indicate similar responses to the organization, such as identification with and comfort in it or alienation and criticism (Scheiberg, 1990, p. 335). Moreover, although the materials convey attributes of the displayer (social roles, pastimes, personal interests, personality traits), they often refer to social conflict, status differences, gender conflicts, and political issues, acknowledgment of which organizations tend to suppress.

By aggregating thematic choices made by individual displayers, an observer can discern socially constructed meaning systems structured through the exhibits that differ from one group to another based on hierarchy, occupation, or other factors. For instance, in their study of office-door cartoon displays in a university, Narasimhan and Pillutla (1994) discovered that those at the bottom of the faculty hierarchy were statistically more likely to engage in this behavior (17.1% of the displayers were assistant professors vs. 5.5% who were full professors), indicating that such displays are a form of "voice" for the hierarchically disadvantaged (in addition, the criticism of hierarchy was one of the recurrent themes in displays). Further, subcultures cohered around occupational rather than departmental groups: Secretaries signaled more of a working-class identity through choices of humorous images, and graduate students combined themes used by academicians and secretaries (articulating their transitional status).

The workspace exhibits are human constructions of personal identity and organizational experiences. People's designed workspaces "speak," communicating sentiments, emotions in and about work, ideas regarding different roles, attitudes toward others, feelings about relationships, and so on. Placement of items is behaviorally significant: What one must concentrate on, what is a source of inspiration or reverie, and what others will see are clearly taken into account. Displays are usually "artful"; aesthetics govern the choice of materials, their combination, and arrangement. Finally, compositions differ in character; one is constrained but pointed, another is ebullient, a third is minimalist. Hence, each exhibits a different style.

The term *style* refers to a distinctive and characteristic mode of presentation, construction, or execution. The concept directs us toward subjective, expressive qualities such as recurrent themes and images, constancies in aesthetic choices, and consistencies in the way people do things. In organizations, much behavior, both individual and collective, becomes stylized, conforming to certain patterns.

Discerning Organizational Style

Workspace decor provides an entry to "organizational style" (see Strati, 1992). In the mid-1980s, I directed a project that documented the nature of work areas in a variety of university departments. Here I mention two contrasting units, described in greater detail by Susan L. Scheiberg (1990), who was a research assistant on the project. Located in a library's basement away from public view, Unit A was responsible for cataloguing. Work areas were open, set off by bookshelves and carts. Furniture was old, drab, and mismatched. The work itself was meticulous and exacting, requiring great concentration. Personal decoration was extravagant, vivacious, wildly imaginative (e.g., souvenirs from trips; large posters of cool, green forests and snow-capped mountains; and even toy spiders and rocket ships dangling from the ceiling). Some examples were transient and changed on a whim while others were more lasting. Individuals spoke of their space (depending on its decor and their mood) as being soothing and relaxing, stimulating and energizing, inspiring, promoting reflection or introspection, or a means of relieving pressure, stress, and feelings of drudgery. Unit B was an administrative financial office in public view. It consisted of identical cubicles partitioned by prefabricated panels in gray and burgundy with standardized nameplates, furniture, and equipment. A storage area in back contained uniform black filing cabinets without so much as a single folder or piece of paper exposed. Inside each cubicle, unseen to visitors, employees had personalized the horizontal surface of their desks, albeit with restraint, displaying coffee mugs, photos of family and pets, and other mementos.

According to Robert W. Witkin's (1990b) essay on organizational style in work relations, organizational style consists of recurring patterns of action that, in turn, structure how people do things. Styles of action "serve to create and to disseminate a unity of *organizational being,*" thereby making the organization "present" and "affective" in the "consciousness and actions of its members" (p. 192). Witkin writes that style is "a set of values defining not only the sensuous/aesthetic qualities with which action is performed, its 'pitch,' 'amplitude,' 'rhythms,' and harmonics,' . . . *but also its more or less enduring patterning, form or structure.*" From this point of view, "we can go on to define the organizational being of an actor as an *incipient readiness* in organizational encounters to realize, in action, a set of organizational values—that is, to cultivate an organizational style" (pp. 193-194).

The cultivation of organizational style is apparent in the university units described above. In regard to Unit B, for instance, even letters and memos from staff, like the typewriters and computers on which they were written, were uniform. All 30 members of the unit agreed about the importance of projecting an image of professionalism to instill in clients feelings of trust and confidence (the director likened the unit to "a bank," often using this and related metaphors in his speech). Employees remarked on a strong sense of teamwork. Said one, "I know that if I get into trouble, anyone here can pick right up and help me out. I'd do it for anyone myself." Several attributed the ability to assist one another to the enforced uniformity. One person said, "Because everything has to be uniform, I can tell just by looking where somebody is. And I can pick right up. It makes things go a lot smoother." All had incorporated the value of standardization into their actions and brought it to bear, as Witkin writes, in various organizational encounters.

Looking for Beliefs in Organizational Photos

Organizational style (i.e., a distinctive and characteristic way of doing things) and also beliefs, assumptions, or meanings can be seen in other symbolic constructions (sometimes folkloric expression in people's interactions, other times symbolism created by the formal organization). This includes architecture, dress (uniform, costume), humor, and the handling of conflicts (see Hatch & Ehrlich, 1993; Rafaeli & Pratt, 1993; Witkin, 1990a, 1990b). Another source is photographs. Organizations produce newsletters, orientation booklets, and other illustrated items for employees as well as annual reports for stockholders and brochures about company products or services for clients. Comparing sets of publications from different organizations is always suggestive (Jones, 1987, pp. 180-184).

Deborah Dougherty and Gideon Kunda (1990, p. 187) infer from a comparison of materials from different companies in the same industry that "the photographs tell a story about the meanings and assumptions of customers shared among organization members." Based on several weeks of scrutinizing 425 photos in the annual reports of five computer equipment manufacturers for a 10-year period, the researchers discovered significant differences in how each company depicts its clients and the company's product for use by the client organization; in other words, what the manufacturer assumes the organizational style of the customer is or, perhaps, what style the manufacturing organization believes the client organization thinks the manufacturer should convey.

An example of differing organizational conceptions of customers is the ways in which three manufacturers portray products with a hospital as the consumer. Digital Equipment Corporation (DEC) emphasizes the enormity and difficulty of client tasks, going so far as to celebrate the large, sweeping scope of these activities. "DEC shows a tense, dramatic moment in the operating room, and suggests a highly technical yet impersonal surgical process," Dougherty and Kunda (1990, p. 191) write. "In contrast to the technological focus, both IBM and Burroughs capture the more ordinary, repetitive aspects of working" (p. 193). IBM emphasizes people doing ordinary work, minimizing the equipment, as in the instance in which smiling nurses conducting a relaxed, simple check-up also comfort the child. "They highlight the service aspects and the human dimensions of hospital care" (p. 193). For Burroughs, the computing equipment is central. "The people are adjuncts to the task of information processing; data going into or coming out of the equipment dominate the scene," as in the hospital in which Burroughs features "information processing rather than service or people" (p. 193). By determining the percentage of photos taken outside or indoors, the gender and ethnicity of workers, the location of employees within the organization, and other matters, Dougherty and Kunda found numerous consistencies that added up to patterns; these in turn suggested beliefs about who the manufacturers' customers are and how their equipment fits into the clients' worlds and styles.

Observing behavior and looking closely at objects, then, whether the objects are created by individuals for themselves or by organizations for employees and clients, can uncover important information about organizational symbolism and the varied modes of meaning making. Another technique, long a primary one in qualitative methods, is interviewing.

4. INQUIRING ABOUT SYMBOLISM, FEELINGS, AND AESTHETICS

Much has been written about ethnographic interviewing (e.g., Bernard, 1988; Ives, 1980; Patton, 1990; Whyte, 1984). Most advice concerns ways to elicit "cultural knowledge" (Fetterman, 1989; Sackmann, 1991; Spradley, 1979; Werner & Schoepfle, 1987). Relatively little has been published in fieldwork manuals on how to query about symbolic behavior, be it about the symbols themselves, the feelings they convey, or the responses they evoke (some exceptions are Briggs, 1986; Goldstein, 1964; Jackson, 1987). In this section, I discuss both direct and indirect questioning. I describe several techniques actually used in ethnographic research; each attempts, with varying degrees of success, to get at symbolism, feelings, or aesthetics.

Questioning Directly

To some extent, direct questioning can yield information about what a person does or has done. This is accomplished by eliciting descriptions of behaviors, actions, activities, and experiences that could have been observed had the researcher been present when they occurred. The interviewer usually asks for an account of, say, a particular event, a specific experience, or a typical day's activities. These have been characterized as "grand-tour" questions (Spradley, 1979; Spradley & McCurdy, 1972; Werner & Schoepfle, 1987).

More specific questions take a variety of forms, one of which is hypothetical; it describes a simulated situation and asks the interviewee to respond to it. Lars Edgren and his team (1990, p. 178) often said to members of a Swedish firm, "Imagine you are reading the newspaper on Sunday morning and suddenly you think you discover a big headline about your company. How does the headline read?" Edgren and his colleagues also queried informants about the company's history, remarkable periods, events of special importance, and who the heroes are (all of which they call "the corporate saga"; see also Clark, 1972). They asked about the rituals of decision making, customary procedures in getting work done, and whether anything was commemorated in a special way (Edgren, 1990, pp. 185-186). Most of these inquiries, then, sought descriptions of symbolic behavior such as stories, rituals, rites, and ceremonials and, to a lesser degree, interpretations of them.

Alan L. Wilkins (1979), in his doctoral dissertation, discusses at length the formal interviewing procedures he used to obtain organizational stories. Interested in how stories function, particularly as embodiments and exemplars of management philosophy, he compared narratives from two companies to explore differences in the extent to which members seem to share a common understanding of and commitment to organizational values.

Wilkins (1979, pp. 170-186) reproduces the interview schedule in its entirety, which I summarize here. The interviewer explained the kind of stories desired—that is, "we are most interested in stories which a good many people would be familiar with" rather than accounts of personal experience. "We call this type of story a group story or an organizational story because most people in a group or organization would know it." Also, "Since every company has both successes and failures, we hope to hear both kinds of stories." The interviewer set up a hypothetical situation, asking the subject to "imagine that I am a friend of yours who doesn't work here and who knows little about the company culture. We are chatting about the company and you really want me to get a feeling for the kind of place you work in. Your only limitation is that you must communicate with me by telling stories about significant events or people in the company or some part of the company. What stories would you tell me?" Later the speaker was asked to imagine that the interviewer was a fellow employee; what stories about well-known events or people would the interviewee tell to an insider during informal chats or work breaks? A maximum of 25 minutes each was devoted to the two hypothetical situations. After telling a story, the interviewee was asked what lesson might be drawn from the tale, does anything in the story apply to you personally, and, "As far as you know, are all of the parts of this story which you did not personally observe factual?"

At the end of 50 minutes, the interviewer turned off the tape recorder, asked a set of questions, and wrote down the answers (Wilkins does not explain why the answers were not taped). Among the 19 questions were those concerning where and from whom the person first learned the story, the situation in which the interviewee last told the story as well as last heard the tale told by someone else (in both cases, noting whether the telling was planned or spontaneous and what the listeners' organizational relationship to the teller was, i.e., subordinates, coworkers, superiors, outsiders), whether the actors in the story were known to the interviewee, and the importance of the story to understanding how the interviewer should regard the company. Last, the interviewee was asked a series of 39 questions about basic demographics (e.g., age, length of time with the company, position, etc.) and such matters as attitudes toward work and other personnel, conception of the company and its philosophy, and organizational commitment.

The interviewers collected 644 stories in 80 interviews lasting up to 2 hours. Wilkins does not reproduce any of the accounts as they were presented (and tape-recorded) during the interviews, although he does give the gist of a few in his own words as part of his narrative about the companies. Because he conceived of story as "script" (a cognitive map), particular themes in story "texts" rather than narrating as a communicative process and social experience assumed priority for Wilkins; he did not observe storytelling in other settings as it occurred naturally, nor did he examine the stylistics and aesthetics of this symbolic behavior. By direct questioning in an interview context, however, he did get many stories of the kind he told respondents he wanted: widely known tales about significant events and people and related to company culture.

Asking Indirectly

We might question individuals directly about something we have observed, requesting explanations of its workings or interpretations of what it means. We can ask about something not witnessed, such as festive events, joking, or food sharing and then leave it at that or try to observe such behaviors in natural settings. Direct questioning may produce data indirectly, for example, unanticipated revelations (interviewees often bring up matters the researcher had not known about or considered important). What I have in mind, however, are enactments of the very symbolic behavior that one seeks, such as narrating or using metaphors.

Because people often give examples of a point they wish to make or describe an event as a basis for the listener to draw inferences, posing certain kinds of questions will likely elicit storytelling behavior. In addition, particular questions may cause interviewees to express themselves with similes and metaphors. Both results may follow from such questions as "What is it like to work here?" "Why is it this way?" "What happens, or fails to happen, because of this?" (Sonduck & Perry, 1983). Some responses to these kinds of questions asked of staff in an academic tutorial unit were the following (Jones, 1987, pp. 135-136): "I joke about this being my second home." "Everyone [supervisors] respects you and your opinion; they treat you like a person." "There's a sense of bonding." "This is a home base." "You feel like you are someone." "People feel protective of one another; they don't want to see anyone get hurt." "People spontaneously do things for one another." "A lot of things happen that bring us closer together." "You can see a sense of unity." "You have a sense of pride in your work." "I feel that what I am doing is important. This is a home base. I value the friends I have made. I have a sense of self-esteem." Images of home, family, community—all with highly positive connotations—dominated the organization members' responses to the question "What's it like to work here?" In other organizations, quite different symbols might emerge in interviewees' statements.

In addition to using metaphors, the interviewees in this unit often exemplified their remarks by describing things that had happened (i.e., they "told stories"), particularly in regard to "Why is it that way?" and "What happens, or fails to happen, because of this?" If they did not voluntarily narrate, or they waited for a cue, then the interviewer's raised eyebrows or "Would you give me an example?" sufficed to bring forth a story.

These three queries, then, are the kinds of direct questions that can produce important data—like symbols and symbolic behavior—indirectly. They usually trigger the act of narrating, with interviewees selecting their own stories to tell, including personal experiences. The questions also produce statements (often loaded with metaphors) that reveal perceptions, attitudes, and meanings that, taken together, constitute a moral and an aesthetic portrait of the organization depicting not only what is deemed right or wrong but also how this makes the person feel, how it affects performance, and what kind of ambience it creates.

Another variation on direct questioning to elicit behaviors indirectly is that of giving limited direction. This is a feature of the "nondirective" or "unstructured" interview (a misnomer, for the interview has a structure, but not a priori; it takes shape as the interviewee talks and the interviewer becomes interested in certain things and suggests directions, however subtly). William Foote Whyte is a master at using degrees of directiveness, from a simple nod of the head and an "uh-huh" or "That's interesting" to stimulating reflection by repeating the informant's remark and adding a question mark ("You didn't feel too good about the job?") to directly asking about something mentioned earlier or raising an entirely new topic (see Whyte, 1984, pp. 99-101; see also Jones, 1991a, on Whyte's methods). His article "Interviewing for Organizational Research" (Whyte, 1953) illustrates the technique well.

Whyte undertook an interview with Columbus Gary in the spring of 1952 during a visit to the Chicago plant of Inland Steel Container Company. Whyte reproduces a portion of the verbatim interview in his article. The 27 minutes of talking take up eight columns in print. There are about 650 words per column, or approximately 5,200 words in the interview (17-20 typewritten pages). The interviewee's comments frequently run half a column, often more. Whyte's longest statement, his first, is only 66 words:

> I'm trying to catch up on things that have happened since I was last here to study this case. That was back in 1950. I think probably the best thing to start would be if you could give your own impressions as to how things are going now, compared to the past. Do you think things are getting better or worse, or staying about the same? (p. 16)

Whyte asked for impressions ("as to how things are going now, compared to the past"), by which he meant Gary's assessments and reactions, and got sentiments—opinions and feelings—followed by (with minimal prompting) a column-long story. Throughout the interview Whyte says such things as "That's a good example. I wonder if you could give me a little more detail," "I see," "That's an interesting one."

Sometimes it is difficult to elicit information directly in interviews, as Whyte (1957) observes elsewhere; one must devise indirect techniques of questioning. The issue arose when Whyte and Frank Miller undertook a study of "The Meaning of Work" at Corning Glass Works. Direct questioning about reactions to the processes involved in work itself (i.e., whether the men "had feelings of creativity") was unproductive (on aesthetics, see also Jones, 1987; Strati, 1990, 1992, 1995). They took an indirect approach by asking an interviewee to arrange a set of cards, each representing a job his team performed, in order of preference. Then they requested an explanation of why he ranked them that way. One gaffer said in regard to pieces that he had ranked high on the preference scale: "When you get done, you've got a nice piece of work there. . . . It really looks like something. . . . When I can say I made that piece, I really swell with pride" (Whyte, 1957, p. 21). Concerning an object he rated at the bottom, another gaffer said, "The trouble with these things is you don't have anything when you're finished. Until they are ground and polished in the finishing room they don't look like anything so it is just a lot of work for nothing" (p. 21).

Whyte concludes his essay by pointing out that having to explain ranking decisions helps interviewees express feelings. Requesting people to make comparisons often produces meaningful responses (i.e., rather than querying how they feel about one thing, ask "How do you feel about *A* compared with *B, C, D*, etc.?"). The presentation of cards or pictures draws attention away from the interviewer and points it toward interviewees' experiences and sentiments:

> Some men seem to find that the device helps them to project themselves imaginatively into the work process. They are then able to verbalize sentiments that might otherwise be difficult to express.... The interviewer may need such special devices to bring out sentiments which the men are not accustomed to verbalizing. (p. 23; on the value of asking "silly" or "outrageous" questions, see Kirk & Miller, 1986, p. 26; on the usefulness of having the interviewee imagine the researcher as a "double," see Gherardi, 1995)

A key element of questioning indirectly, as Whyte suggests, is having interviewees project themselves imaginatively into situations. For instance, Antonio Strati (1990, p. 208) asked informants, "If I were your double, what could I do?" In their research on Canadian banks, Beck and Moore (1985, pp. 351-353) presented managers with a forced-choice selection of metaphors (see also Edgren, 1990, p. 186), asking them to choose an appropriate metaphor and discuss its application. The metaphor set for the bank's internal status system, for example, consisted of "sponge, string of beads, hammer and nail, sun and planets, staircase, beehive, family." Several managers selected the "family" metaphor; their explanations of the choice reflected confidence in order, hierarchy, and unity (p. 343). Said one, "The manager is a father/mother figure and so on down the line. Every member of the staff feels part of the family on an equal basis. There is leadership plus a family unit at the same time" (p. 343). Others chose the sun and planets, a beehive, or a staircase, with explanations again emphasizing centrality, benevolent authority, and hierarchy. One example is a manager's statement that "the branch has a queen bee, drones and workers. Everybody has his position. Sort of an autonomous organization, getting policy from above. And the manager is benevolent" (p. 343). This technique, along with other procedures, enabled Beck and Moore to collect information about cultural imagery at various levels (from the national societal context to the banking milieu to specific local managerial cultures). There are other psychological projective techniques for obtaining qualitatively rich data for sociological use. One involves "running a commentary on imaginatively re-lived events," developed by Witkin and Poupart (1986, p. 79) and discussed below.

Requesting Commentary on Relived Events

The researcher can ask "feeling questions" directly as a way of trying to tap the affective dimension of organizational life (Patton, 1990, p. 291). In direct questioning, the interviewer seeks adjective responses: "To what extent do you feel . . . [anxious, happy, sad, confident, afraid, etc.]?" or "How did that [comment, situation, experience, etc.] make you feel?" But missing from most responses are the sense of immediacy, depth or intensity of feeling, and complexity of feelings that events often evoke.

Symbolic behavior, particularly folklore, usually incites feelings in speaker and listener. Recall from the discussion of the emotional power of symbols (see Chapter 1) how Hirschhorn reacted upon hearing that a company president and controller were "nickel-and-diming" the units to death and his having to "brown bag it" at a retreat he was hired to lead; Hirschhorn immediately felt the emotions that other members of the organization experienced.

Like figurative speech, storytelling excites emotions. The narrator relives the event and the audience participates through the speaker's gestures, facial expressions, metaphors, sharp delineation of characters, and dramatization of actions. Often the storyteller laces the description with commentary on how it felt (or feels) to be involved in the event described. Not infrequently, the narrator begins with the past tense but quickly switches to the present, which places the speaker in the center of the action and gives the listener a ringside seat.

Witkin and Poupart (1986) base their running commentary technique on similar observations. What good storytellers do, write the authors, is "intensify the intimate present-centered quality of the events they are communicating" by slipping into the present tense, bringing the listener into the heart of the scene. This is "an important communicative device in everyday life, particularly when one seeks to communicate directly the sensuous and affective dimension of lived experience" (p. 79). In a pilot study researching community social work groups in Quebec, including abortion clinics, Witkin and Poupart developed an interview technique that has the respondent provide a running commentary on her description of an imaginatively relived event. Witkin (1990b) later used it in a study of organizational style in work relations. The procedure seeks to reproduce some of the features of naturally occurring folkloric behavior (found in narrating, using metaphors, etc.), but this time in an interview setting; it focuses on feelings, bringing them to the fore and making them "visible" to (and experienced by) the researcher (see also Höpfl & Linstead, 1993).

The interviewee is asked to recount an occurrence, but to do so in the present rather than past tense and to provide a running commentary on the emotions experienced in the event described. Talented narrators usually do this, but not everyone delivers virtuosic performances, and certainly not always in an interview context (often, the authors write, interviewees tend to act as lay scientists, trying to analyze and evaluate actions in terms of some theory of knowledge rather than just describe what they experienced, how it affected them, and what their thoughts and feelings were). Hence, Witkin and Poupart found it necessary to "train" interviewees, first by giving an example themselves, then by asking for discourse on a nonsensitive event before finally requesting descriptions of key encounters in the cultural life of the organization (which can be contextualized and compared to get at larger sociological questions about modal tendencies, distributions and differences within social groups, etc.).

For example, a doctor in an abortion clinic on her first attempt at using this technique briefly characterized her journey by Metro to the place of the interview. Her description was flat, in the past tense, and devoid of commentary on how she felt (not surprising, considering the "unnaturalness" of interview settings). With some coaxing from Witkin and Poupart, however, she gathered her thoughts and began again. This time she spoke in considerable detail about what she was doing as well as what she was thinking at particular moments. Still, there was little expression of emotion, perhaps because of the unremarkableness of her journey. Later, however, the doctor told of just having heard at a planning meeting that a close colleague had decided to stop performing abortions. Here was a topic more central to what Witkin and Poupart were interested in and one that had an emotional impact on the doctor. Below is the authors' edited excerpt, which they present as an illustration of "the live contact with the affective dimension in the work process that can be elicited" with their technique.

Helen announces officially that she will not do any more abortions from now on. She is getting off and I react very negatively. I feel like I am being abandoned. I also often think of stopping, but I was never able to do it, and Helen does it and stops. I tell everybody that I accept it but it is obvious that I don't accept it. . . . I am mad. I am disappointed, I am aggressive, and I have a lot of sadness, and it's all these feelings at the same time. I am really upset. I can feel my heart beating. . . . It confirms that I was working with her side by side without knowing what was going on in her head. We were there physically side by side but that's all. . . . I feel a lot of resentment, there's all this thing about our fighting together for abortion and a lack of communication, and we did not share all the road she has travelled mentally. It's like a lack of trust and a lack of confidence, and suddenly "bang" she says she is quitting. . . . (p. 84)

In this account, told entirely in the present tense about an event that occurred in the recent past, the doctor expresses disappointment, anger, a sense of abandonment, a feeling of betrayal, sadness, frustration, aggression, and resentment. She also conveys *why* she experienced these feelings. She uses emotionally charged language: "like I am being abandoned," "I can feel my heart beating [pounding]," "suddenly 'bang'. . . ." These are traditional expressions, examples of folkloric behavior that not only distill her feelings into symbols but also provoke emotions in the listener. Moreover, the experience she had and her reaction to it involve aesthetics.

The word *aesthete* derives from the Greek *aisthētē,* "one who perceives form" (Jones, 1987, p. 172). *Aesthetic* comes from the adjective *aisthetikos,* "capable of sensory perception" (Forrest, 1988, p. 22). The term *aesthetics* refers to sensory perception, the experience of sensations, and responses to the stimulus. The source of an aesthetic experience may be any event, product, or performance perceived by the senses and that has affect. An aesthetic experience and responses to it are marked by noticeable physical sensations, strongly felt emotions, and a heightened awareness of the perceived form. For example, Rachel Fretz-Yoder (1981) quotes a listener remarking on a performance: "The storyteller tells the story in a way that makes you feel it in your body. The blood rushes to your head or feet, your scalp tingles, and it feels like your hair is pulled tight." The excellent narrator "can move his audience deeply," writes Fretz-Yoder (p. 26). "Perhaps this is what we mean by an aesthetic experience—that we have sensations and feelings as a result of hearing something so vividly presented."

The experience need not be pleasurable or the reaction positive to be aesthetic within the "affective dimension" of organizations. The doctor's response to her colleague's surprising (and to her, disconcerting) announcement at the planning meeting was highly negative. As in the case of a positive response, however, she experienced strong emotions and notable physiological sensations. She identifies at least eight emotions by name. Also, her body reacts: "I can feel my heart beating." Her feelings of betrayal and abandonment were probably accompanied by other physiological sensations, such as a tightening in the abdomen (i.e., "a sickening feeling"), a weight pressing down on her, perhaps difficulty swallowing, and so on. As the listeners, Witkin and Poupart were affected by her performance, experiencing with her some of the same emotions and physical sensations that she felt and therefore gaining insights into the meaning of actions and events for an organization member.

Shoshana Zuboff (1988) used a different kind of imaginative projection to probe the affective dimension of organizational experience, having interviewees draw their "felt sense" of their jobs. Like the running commentary on a relived event, this procedure brought forth aesthetic responses and conveyed emotions that otherwise might not have been apparent in the interview setting and helped her understand shared meanings.

Drawing Feelings

Zuboff conducted research on the introduction of advanced information technology to clerical work, an innovation equal in its consequences to the Industrial Revolution. Clerks found it difficult to adapt to the shift from pencil-and-paper processing to computerization, with the attendant displacement of traditional patterns of interaction and communication, disruption of familiar social routines, and alteration in workspace that isolated the individual from others. Complaints about the work were expressed symbolically as bodily suffering. "During my discussions with these office workers, I sometimes asked them to draw pictures that represented their 'felt sense' of their job experience before and after the conversion to the new computer system" (Zuboff, 1988, p. 141). Although a psychological projective technique, requesting drawings of feelings had sociological import in uncovering the changing social and cultural patterns in the organization and the meanings they wrought. Zuboff writes,

> One group of pictures (the largest) illustrated a single theme: the various forms of bodily alteration resulting from the new conditions of work, including hair loss; impaired eyesight; contortion of facial muscles; radical decrease in bodily dimensions; rigidification of the torso, arms, and faces; inability to speak or hear; immobility; headaches; and enforced isolation. (p. 141)

The clerks drew upon a traditional repertoire of symbols, portraying themselves "as chained to desks, surrounded by bottles of aspirin, dressed in prison stripes, outfitted with blinders," and faceless. Two sketches by a benefits analyst incorporate several conventions to depict changes in herself and her interactional routines. In the first drawing, she speaks to a caller: "Hi, this is Ann. Can I help you?" A large poster or painting adorns the wall; a cup sits on the edge of her desk near the phone. Behind her reposes a worker, next to whom is a picture of a shining sun, two frolicking people, and a tree. The clerk's second drawing (p. 144) consists of only one person, shown as a stick figure, three strands of hair standing upright, staring blankly at a computer screen. The clerk said,

> "I used to have someone behind me in case I needed to tell them about this irate phone call. But now there isn't anybody there. Now she is stiff. She is all by herself. You feel stiff. You're just out there."

"A second group of drawings by the clerks and their supervisors illustrate the isolation of the individual office worker and this new sense of distance between the clerical function and those who supervise it," Zuboff writes (p. 151). A dental claims supervisor drew a "before" picture of a large circle in which there are nine smaller circles, three in each of three horizontal rows, with a slightly larger circle at the top. The "after" drawing consists of six randomly placed squares with a small circle off to the side. She commented,

> "Before, we were all pulling files. You knew everyone. And now it is, like, everybody has their own desk and they do not really need me. They kind of do their job. They need me for questions they cannot handle, but for the most part, a girl can come in all day and not ask me anything and go home at night. I do not feel they are as close to me as we were before, and they are not as close with each other. Not that the office should be like a party, but before we were more of a family." (Zuboff, 1988, p. 153)

Here, note the metaphor of "family" and possible symbolic meanings associated with circle and box or square.

To summarize, researchers sometimes ask questions directly about the symbolism in an organization and the sentiments that a condition arouses. A less direct technique for eliciting symbolic behavior is to ask questions regarding what it is like to work in the organization and why it is that way, which may induce an interviewee to narrate and use metaphors or similes. Requesting rankings and comparisons is another. A third technique employs imaginative projections, from requiring interviewees to choose a metaphor and explain why it aptly describes organizational structure or process to commenting on a relived experience or drawing feelings and a felt sense of the organization. The goal is to uncover organizational symbolism, its sources, meanings, and significance. In having interviewees draw feelings, for example, Zuboff was able to elicit psychological responses to social and cultural changes in organizations; she also documented the personal use of traditional symbols related to individuals' organizational experiences. Observing behavior and interviewing organization members are only part of the documentation process, however. Another involves making records of symbolic behavior that serve as the basis for interpretation.

5. RECORDING PERFORMANCES VERSUS RECONSTRUCTING TEXTS

Sometimes researchers audiotape (rarely videotape) interviews or other symbolic events and performances; often they do not. Because they think taping is unnecessary, the equipment is not at hand, they feel uncomfortable using it, or cameras and tape recorders are discouraged, they take notes during an interview or try to reconstruct the symbolic behavior from memory. This raises methodological and epistemological questions about the nature of documentation and interpretations of it. How do the records differ? What information can various modes of documentation capture? How is meaning constructed, and by whom? In sum, what constitutes the database, what can you do with it, and what do you present as the symbols, symbolic constructions, and symbolic performances?

Taped Narrating Compared to Story Reports and Reconstructions

To compare and contrast different kinds of records, I draw on research by Wendy Caesar (1975), wife of the assistant manager to the Detroit Symphony Orchestra, who elicited 200 stories from 32 musicians in seven interviews (during a week on the road) and sporadically when opportunity permitted. She tape-recorded some performances and jotted down the essence of others, noted informants' reports about stories, and reconstructed several narratives from memory. Eight examples of stories and narrating treat an event involving Fritz Reiner, who fired a musician for appearing to mock his diminutive movements while conducting the orchestra.

Example "A" of narrating, which Caesar tape-recorded and then transcribed, is the following:

[A] So what happened was—we were on tour—it was the last night out—and we were in Lancaster, Pennsylvania. And all of a sudden I looked—I never look in the back of the orchestra. I mean, you'll never—when you see me—when you see the orchestra on stage, you will *never* see me—if anything happens, you will never see me turn around to see what happened, because I consider that unprofessional. I just wouldn't do anything—my eyes are always in the front. I know what's happening back there—I can hear for myself, y'know, but I don't go looking around. Anyhow—but I looked at Reiner— nothing had happened that you could *hear* but something obviously had happened because he was looking back this way to the basses and [face of fury] WRAAN [shaking head] like—you could tell. . . . [WDC—Could you hear him?] No, you couldn't hear anything but you could tell by the way the mouth—the way it was going—that he was definitely swearing. And I couldn't figure out what happened, because I didn't hear anything wrong—nobody did anything wrong. So the next day we got on the train going back to Pittsburgh. And there's this bass player coming along in the train and in his vest pocket of his coat he had some—a little bulge and something sticking out. So I asked him as he passed by, "What do y'have there?" He says, "Oh, I have a spyglass." So he pulled it out—some 59 cent spyglass—you buy it in Rexall Drugs or something like that. And he says—he was a very nervous individual—played the bass—and he said—oh, you know Reiner had a notoriously—a very small beat. He never—very—I mean, he did move his hands in large motions like this [waving arms] but he also, a lot of times, had a small beat. So [this musician] said, "Couldn't see the beat, couldn't see the beat." So he took out the spyglass—he stopped playing the bass, took out the spyglass—at a *concert*—and was looking through the spyglass at Reiner. Naturally, Reiner got mad at him, see, and so he started to swear and that was it—that's the last time he played for him. He was fired right away—we never saw the kid in the orchestra. When we got back to Pittsburgh—that was in Lancaster, Pennsylvania—I think in the book there he put it somewhere else, but it was in Lancaster, it was on tour—and he threw him out, that's all. That was the end of that. (pp. 86-87)

A second example (which Caesar did not tape-record) is a report by an informant about a story concerning Reiner rather than an act of narrating itself.

[B] There's one about Fritz Reiner—this is a classic—you've heard this one. He had a very tiny beat and one of the bass players during a concert set up a telescope and [peering motions]. He was fired at once, of course. I think he's in Dallas now. This is *absolutely true*—you can ask [another Detroit player] about it—I think he knows the name of the bass player. (p. 87)

Caesar also includes the following text that she reconstituted from notes on a narrating event:

[C] Reiner had a very small beat, all in about two inches, so one of the basses hated his guts and one night he brought in a huge ship's telescope. During a rehearsal—no, I think it was a concert—there was Reiner [conducting motions] and—can you imagine?—he looked over and there is this big telescope [gestures of looking through huge telescope and sweeping the scene]. Of course, the guy was fired on the spot. Reiner was one of the last of the old-style autocrats. (p. 87)

As Caesar's examples illustrate, an informant's report ("B") and the researcher's reconstructed text ("C") are far briefer than a taped narrating that has been faithfully transcribed ("A"). The latter includes the narrator's gestures, voice qualities, colloquialisms typical of informal speaking, and even digressions. The transcription reminds us that in narrating, a storyteller pauses, makes asides, repeats ideas or descriptions of action, uses "fillers," checks the audience's interest and understanding, and alters intonation and inflection (Ellis, 1987; Fine, 1984; Georges, 1969; Riessman, 1993; Van Maanen, 1988, p. 109). The narrator communicates not only verbally but also paralinguistically by means of laughter, tone of voice, pitch, rate, and stress; through kinesics such as posture, gestures, and facial expressions; and by proxemics, coming closer to or moving away from a listener, even touching someone (see Bauman, 1977; Fine, 1984). Channels of communication include the following:

Aural Channels (Linguistic and Paralinguistic)

Vocal characterizers (noises one talks through, e.g., laughing, whispering, yelling, crying)

Vocal qualifiers (intensity, pitch, tone, inflection, cadence)

Vocal segregates (sounds such as "uh-huh," "uh-uh," "uh")

Voice qualities (modifications of language and vocalizations, e.g., pitch, articulation, rhythm, resonance, tempo)

Idiom (dialect, colloquialisms, jargon, slang)

Discourse markers ("well," "but," "so," "okay")

Stylistic devices (use of repetition, formulaic expressions, parallelism, figurative language, onomatopoeia, pauses, silences, mimicry)

Kinesics, Proxemics, and Artifactual Channels

Facial expressions (smile, frown, furrowed brow)

Gestures (nodding, arm motions, hand movements)

Shift in posture

Alterations in positioning from intimacy (touching) to social or public distance

The performance space (e.g., an allocated room or impromptu in a corridor, rearranged seating, etc.)

Props (especially for ceremonial oratory)

Clothing, cosmetics, and even fragrance (e.g., incense)

In contrast to information-rich transcriptions, reports and reconstituted texts provide little more than a skeletal plot summary. They translate first-person, subjective, and affective narrative performances into third-person, "objective" accounts (Babcock, 1977, p. 64). A reconstructed text, even if it consists of some of the narrator's phrases, is composed by the researcher based on notes and memory in an effort to make sense of what happened; it is the researcher's story, not the narrator's.

With rare exceptions, the literature on organizational culture and symbolism focuses on stories, not narrating performances. Only "texts" ("artifacts") are presented and interpreted. These consist of brief summaries, reports, reconstructions, edited versions lacking the narrator's asides and digressions as well as nonverbal or paralinguistic behavior, and sometimes researchers' own reworking of multiple tellings into a "meta-story" presented as "the organizational narrative." Pronouncements about meaning are based on these kinds of records. But whose meaning is it? What are the sources of meaning? And how does a narrator, in interaction with an audience, construct meaning?

Sources of Meanings in Performance

Data from Caesar's article indicate several sources of meaning making when people narrate organizational experiences. These include the narrator, the stylistics of performance, asides or digressions, and context. All influence "the story" that a narrator tells, the manner of doing so, and meanings that are generated in the narrating event.

THE NARRATOR

Recall that the accounts documented by Caesar refer to an orchestra member's being fired for using a magnifying device to see conductor Fritz Reiner's diminutive movements better. Story reports and reconstructed texts add little to this. Apparent in the transcriptions of four narratings that

Caesar tape-recorded, however, is that narrators provide motivation and interpretation. It is through such techniques that they construct, often while they speak, a logic to behavior and events and make it meaningful. Narrator "A" (quoted earlier) implies the bassist intended no disrespect; he was trying as best he could to follow Reiner's direction. According to narrator "D," the bassist wanted out of his contract because of the oppressive climate (characteristic of the industry historically, he indicates, and particularly of the Pittsburgh Symphony at this time under Reiner's direction). For narrator "F," the bassist was a "wise guy" who subsequently "had a hard time living down the whole bit." Narrator "G" says that Reiner "had been picking on" the bassist, who precipitated the firing so he could flaunt his decision by saying, "No, you're wrong; I *quit* yesterday," and then waving his train ticket.

Caesar does not provide biographical information about the narrators, so we do not know why they imputed the motivations to the bassist that they describe. Nevertheless, the fact that in four narratings there are four different explanations of what occurred and why it happened indicates that an organizational story does not have a single meaning among those who tell it. And because the interpretation differs from one narrator to another, personality factors and the individual's experiences must play a significant role in the construction of the story and what it means to them on this occasion of telling it.

THE STYLISTICS OF NARRATING

In each of the four instances of narrating, the speaker employs dramatization (gestures, facial expressions, sounds), repetition, and dialogue. Narrators "D," "F," and "G" set the event at a rehearsal, allowing for verbal exchanges between characters, an aesthetic device that "heightened the immediacy and dramatic nature of the confrontation," writes Caesar (1975, pp. 89-90). Narrator "A" says it happened at a public concert, a "much more unthinkable moment." But Narrator "A" incorporates dialogue by employing another technique—that of telling a story within a story; the next day on the train, he says, he asked the bass player to explain his actions at the concert.

The dramatizations, especially the verbal exchanges, lend credibility that the event actually occurred and affect the listener's assumptions and interpretations, a second source of meaning making. Narrator "A" goes so far as to correct a published account regarding the city where it transpired, and in his story he even converses with the bassist about the incident.

Whether the event happened at all may be open to question; as we have seen, who did what with which and why vary with the tellings by different narrators. Narrator "A" might or might not have been present; putting oneself close to or even in the midst of the action is a common aesthetic and logical feature of narrating (Young, 1987). However, his narrative claim of being there convinced Caesar that his account is the progenitor of all others (the "normalform" that establishes the "type"; see Georges & Jones, 1995), for she quotes it first, seems to regard it as "true," and writes that in other versions the scene *"became* a rehearsal instead of a concert" and the spyglass *"became* binoculars" (emphasis added), as though other narratings must have been based on this one. In other words, through the stylistics of performance, the narrator has constructed an organizational occurrence, given meaning to it, and influenced the researcher's interpretations.

ASIDES AND DIGRESSIONS

Narrator "A" dwells on himself in a lengthy aside at the very beginning of his narrating. " 'And all of a sudden I looked—I never look in the back of the orchestra,' " he says. " I mean, you'll never—when you see me—when you see the orchestra on stage, you will *never* see me—if anything happens, you will never see me turn around to see what happened, because I consider that unprofessional.' " This aside presents a strong organizational value, that of professionalism, and it describes a norm for behavior symbolizing this value: not looking behind you when performing on stage.

After starting to tell the story about Reiner and the bassist, narrator "D" digresses, characterizing the music industry not only in the United States but also historically in Europe, relating it to political events. He also sets up a comparison between the organizational climate in the Pittsburgh Symphony under Reiner's autocratic direction and the Dallas orchestra where the bassist has gotten a job.

"You know Reiner was a very authoritarian man and a very difficult man with which to deal. [another story omitted here] So under—you think—in this kind of atmosphere poor [____] had just about *had* it, he couldn't take it any longer. It was just a bit too repressive for him. (Just as I saw in the program notes to this past week of concerts, Luciano Berio said that in 1945 he heard Schoenberg, Bartók, Webern, Hindemith—all these people—for the *first time,* at the age of nineteen. And that's when he realized how oppressive had been the Fascism under which he had been living in Italy.) At any rate, I guess you might say it was this same oppressive, somewhat Fascistic type of atmosphere that—that

so impressed itself (or *de*pressed itself) [chuckle] on [this man's] mentality. So
he wanted to get out of the orchestra. . . . (p. 88)

Narrator "A's" aside constitutes a third of his narrating, and "D's"
digression comprises about 40% of his story (not to mention that he told
another story before finishing the one he had started). Important information and meanings lie in asides and seeming digressions (Georges, 1983;
Riessman, 1993, p. 57). These elements are never included in mere reports
about stories, they are seldom noted by the researcher jotting down a story,
and they are usually lacking in edited versions of published texts (Georges,
1995). Seemingly "extraneous" to the story plot, they nevertheless are a
crucial aspect of narrating, for they bring historical and cultural background, personal and organizational values, point of view, and interpretations of events.

CONTEXT

Narrators digress and make asides, comment on one thing but not
another, go into greater or less detail because they are responding to the
immediate context involving themselves and their listener(s). This includes
identities, status relationships, and assumptions about what the listener
knows and understands.

Wendy Caesar was the wife of the assistant manager of the Detroit
Symphony interviewing the orchestra for examples of folklore. "Not only
was I an outsider (non-musician), but also I was on the wrong side of the
fence," she writes. "There is an unfortunate and sometimes bitter orches-
tra-management tension in the air, especially when contract negotiations
approach" (1975, p. 91). She pointedly avoided asking for stories about the
Detroit Symphony, but interviewees were always aware of Caesar's status
as a nonmusician "management wife" conducting research (she also notes
that they reacted to her as a woman, not telling her ribald stories that they
told one another).

Given this situation, it is not surprising that narrator "A" engages in
"impression management" (Goffman, 1959), going to considerable length
to explain and justify his behavior and impress on her his adherence to
professional standards. Because so much of the narrating by "D" consists of
a digression about the oppressive climate of the industry and the authoritarian manner of Fritz Reiner, he probably was assuming ignorance on the
part of Caesar, a nonmusician, and therefore explained circumstances so
that she could better envision and vicariously experience the incident.

Symbolic Construction of
Organization in Situated Events

Caesar's examples indicate kinds of information missing from story reports and reconstructions: biographical, stylistic, contextual, and the seemingly extraneous (asides and digressions). But these, rather than story "texts" (plot outlines) are principal sources of interpretations for those involved in the narrating event. If they are realms of meaning making by participants, then presumably researchers' documentation and presentation should include them as well.

Caesar's examples also suggest that symbolic behavior such as narrating is "situated" in time and space; its nature, messages, and meanings are affected by immediate circumstances involving the identities of narrator(s) and listener(s) and their status and personal relationships, concerns, viewpoints, reasons for being together, and so forth. Out of the confluence of these a narrative is generated, its interpretations particular to this occasion (although frequently there are similarities across events; e.g., the various accounts of Reiner all appear to concern issues of leadership and power).

Sometimes the narrating constructs an organization. Caesar's data offer hints of this in narrator "A's" aside about organizational behavioral norms and "D's" digression into industry history and organizational climate and leadership style. In an essay on "the storytelling organization," David M. Boje (1991b) examines the process by which participants construct the organization—in this case, an office supply firm.

Boje's data demonstrate several features of narrating. Although some people excel at "storytelling," even becoming "raconteurs," narrating occurs not just as a specialized act by a recognized specialist but frequently in conversation as people interact. Even though someone else assumes the role of narrator, listeners become coproducers through their comments, questions, and reactions. They may even take over the narrating started by another person, adding details to what happened, supplying background information, or offering explanations. After someone has narrated, a listener may "gloss" the story, imputing meaning according to his or her own understanding and rhetorical intent.

As narrating occurs in the course of conversation, there are false starts, interruptions, brief allusions to an event (Boje calls them "terse stories"), and talking over someone else.

To try to capture interruptions, hesitation, and intonation, Boje employed the following conventions (Boje, 1991b, p. 112; see also Ellis, 1987; Fine, 1984):

//	Overlapping talk from the first to the last slash. Utterances begin with an upper-case letter and end with a period.
. . .	A pause of 1 second or less within an utterance.
(2.0)	A pause of more than 1 second within an utterance or between turns; the number indicates the length of the pause.
* * *	A deletion.
[ ]	An explanatory insertion.
Italics	A word or part of a word emphasized by a speaker.
?	A question, marked by a rise in pitch.
!	An exclamation, marked by a rise in pitch or intense body language.

Turning to Boje's examples, I quote one to illustrate the nature of narrating as well as to show how participants construct (or reconstruct) the organization in regard to its purpose in the past and its direction in future. The narrating concerns the founding of Goldco. The company is 35 years old, has 300 employees, and has over $50 million in annual sales. It has seen five CEOs in the past 2 years and is being acquired by its second conglomerate. Doug (the current CEO) and the vice-presidents—Sam, Ruth, Jim, Mike, Harmon, and Kora—have gathered in a hotel room to strategize about the fate of various divisions in the coming acquisition. A comment by the CEO precipitates narrating by Sam, followed by the CEO's gloss.

Doug: * * * I look at Goldco as a toy that	1154
somebody decided to put in the company	1155
because it was fun and it also brought	1156
in/	1157
Sam: Well/I'll tell you how that came	1158
about	1159
Doug: I thought you would (lots of laughter	1160
from the group)	1161
Sam: Sam Coche worked for Sea Breeze or	1162
something like that, oh you know the	1163
story?	1164
Doug: No go ahead tell it, really it's	1165
important.	1166
Sam: He got out there and he came over and	1167
they formed Goldco and Goldco does	1168
not mean Gold Company or anything	1169
else they took the first four	1170

initials from Billy Gold, which is	1171
G O L D and from Coche and that's how	1172
they got Goldco.	1173

Doug: And it was a good living for a couple | 1174
of people. It was a nice toy for | 1175
Billy, he made a few bucks on the | 1176
thing. He had some fun for it but | 1177
then the motivation at that time was a | 1178
whole lot different than it is today. | 1179
We don't have the luxury of screwing | 1180
around with something like that/(lots | 1181
of cross talk at this point)/ | 1182

(Returns to turn-by-turn talk.)

During the course of conversation and turn-by-turn talk, Sam, who has served longest at Goldco and was an eyewitness to its early beginnings, assumes the social personae of narrator (Georges, 1969, 1990), saying at a timely and appropriate moment (Georges, 1987), "I'll tell you how that came about" (lines 1158-1159). Doug, the current CEO, good-naturedly grants him this role (1160-1161). Even though Doug knows how the company was founded, he encourages Sam to give the history: "No go ahead tell it; really, it's important." Sam employs opening and closing formulae to mark his narrating performance: "I'll tell you how that came about" and "that's how they got Goldco" (lines 1158-1159, 1172-1173). Doug narrates to some extent, largely as "glosses" to what Sam has described. These consist of colloquialisms, figures of speech, and metaphors that evoke vivid images and strong emotions: "a good living for a couple of people" and "a nice toy for Billy" who "made a few bucks on the thing" as compared to today when "we don't have the luxury of screwing around." He concentrates on a leading character, employs the technique of contrast or opposition (the polarity of the company as a toy for "Billy" versus the business strategy required today), and creates memorable tableaux (Billy with his plaything).

Participants behave symbolically in several ways that generate meaning. First of all, they hold the meeting at a time and location away from the workplace, symbolically (and instrumentally) separating it from the usual concerns and activities at work. Doug, rather than a vice-president, leads the session, a symbolic expression of his position as CEO and intention to direct the reorganization. He uses humor, a strategy often employed to ease tensions and create the impression of an easy give-and-take to encourage the free exchange of opinions and ideas (Arora, 1988, p. 187). Doug defers to a long-time member's knowledge and expertise, conveying a sense of respect. Even though he knows the history, having someone else tell the basic story of Goldco's founding before Doug gives his own interpretation of it has the effect of suggesting that his attribution of meaning is shared by others. As he glosses Sam's story and adds to Sam's narrating, the CEO employs traditional expressions that excite emotions and dramatize his message. He also uses rhetorical strategies typical of epic narratives (Olrik, 1909), setting up a strongly demarcated polarity and creating memorable tableaux.

In narrative collaboration with Sam, Doug conveys his conception of the company's past and justifies his beliefs about how and why the organization must change in his effort to influence others' interpretations and behavior. Other examples documented by Boje demonstrate that the vice-presidents concur with the CEO's vision because in their narrating (e.g., p. 116, involving Ruth, Kora, and Sam with Doug present) they reconstruct the past, reinterpret leaders' abilities and effectiveness, illustrate an organization rampant with paranoia, and defend the need for new policies. They "construct the organization" narratively by virtue of what event(s) they choose to describe, the logic they give to others' activities, and the inferences they make about how things ought to be.

As Helen B. Schwartzman (1988, p. 91) writes and Boje's data illustrate, symbolic behavior such as narrating is "a form for individual interpretation, construction, and reconstruction of events" and a way for people "to create and then discover the meaning of what it is they are doing and saying" (see also McCall, 1990). Organization is found in acts of symbolism through which experience is shaped, understood, and communicated to oneself and others. Meanings unfold in the performance event as people find, invent, or elaborate patterns and fit them to current situations to make sense of the past and present or to model the future (Boje, 1991b, pp. 109, 113).

Perceiving these processes and conveying them to others requires information-rich documentation. This is not to contend that in research or consultation every narrating, instance of using proverbial expressions, or example of customary or ritualistic behavior must be audio- or videotaped, transcribed, analyzed, and presented. But neither should the researcher nor the consultant depend exclusively on reports and reconstructions. To understand how people construct meanings through symbolic behavior and to know what these multiple interpretations are, sometimes one must have documentation that includes information about the participants (personality, experiences, present concerns, relationships to one another), the immediate circumstances of their interaction, the multiple channels of communication (verbal, paralinguistic, kinesics, artifactual), and details of what they said and did. "By displaying text in particular ways, we provide grounds for our arguments, just like a photographer guides the viewer's eye with lenses and by cropping images," writes Riessman (1993, p. 13) about narrative analysis. Different kinds of records and transcriptions result in "and support different interpretations and ideological positions, and they ultimately create different worlds" (Riessman, 1993, p. 13). This leads to another consideration in the study of organizational symbolism, that of the part played by the researcher when documenting, interpreting, and presenting it.

6. BEING AWARE OF
THE SYMBOLICS OF RESEARCH

"It is neatly the case that persons under the eye of an avowed researcher may well act in ways knowledgeable of this fact," writes John Van Maanen (1991, p. 31). "While researchers attend to the study of other persons and their activities, these others attend to the study of researchers and their activities." The process of interpreting the researcher and constructing meanings about the research is often a symbolic one; it begins when the research is announced or even before (Georges & Jones, 1980, pp. 23-42). Roger Culler, Jack Santino's intermediary to other telephone company employees whose stories he sought at the meeting of the Central Office Club, told Santino (1978b, p. 39), "When you go out there, tell them that it's for the Smithsonian. That you're with the Working Americans project, and it's for the Smithsonian. Make sure you mention the Smithsonian when you tell them about your project." Stating three times in quick succession that Santino should associate himself with the Smithsonian Institution was a symbolic act by Culler, who clearly was trying to "tell" Santino something about the symbolic import of associating himself with a prestigious organization. Culler apparently sensed that such affiliation would lend credibility to a project about storytelling, whose seriousness or value might otherwise be doubted, and therefore help elicit participation in the research.

The Researcher as Symbol

Through their self-introductions, field-workers influence the ways in which their selected subjects conceive them. Labels that researchers assign to themselves or imply through their descriptions of their interests always evoke reactions and interpretations from others (Georges & Jones, 1980, pp. 53-57). Karen Stephenson (1990; all quotes below are from pp. 248-260) captures the symbolics of initiating research in her report about a recently formed information systems division of a company. She gained access through an intermediary who told the CEO ("Sanders") of "U.S.Tek" and the president ("Tiner") of the "Softek" division that she was an anthropologist studying corporate settings to understand how individuals make decisions. Satisfied with her responses to questions about her background and research, the president agreed to the project, welcoming her to what he called his "village-size tribe" (a metaphor presumably chosen to express his understanding of anthropological research). The CEO "commented that if I had been an MBA student or a sociologist I wouldn't have gotten past the door. He said, 'You're here because you're an anthropologist.'"

Stephenson was to introduce herself to the 200-member division at its quarterly meeting. After running through the agenda, the president flipped to the next slide, which read:

SPECIAL ANNOUNCEMENT

NEWS FLASH
   U.S.TEK tribe to be studied by antropologist. Customs, rituals and communication between tribe members will be part of the study to be carried out on this well-known high tech tribe.

"Suddenly, I noticed that anthropologist had been misspelled as 'antropologist,'" writes Stephenson. The president, who had not spotted the error, invited her to come to the stage. On reaching the front of the room, Stephenson said to the audience, "Well, it seems to me that if you're going to have an anthropologist on site, then the first order of business is to learn how to spell the word properly." This, she writes, "seemed to diffuse a potentially tense situation." She then described herself and her research in general terms, explaining "that I would come to work everyday, spend a full working day at the office, attend meetings, assist in non-technical mundane tasks, if it were helpful, as well as conduct interviews with a majority of the employees" and assuring them of confidentiality (p. 257)— in other words, behave (symbolically) like a researcher. Stephenson was given a private office in which to conduct interviews, a symbolic space. "As a gesture of acceptance, my name was placed on the company's phone list as their 'Visiting Anthropologist' " (p. 258). In sum, both Stephenson and her sponsors interacted through expressive forms and did so largely in terms of the symbolism and meanings surrounding her identity as an anthropological researcher.

The Symbolics of Data Gathering

Symbolism and meaning making continue throughout research. Recall that Duncan (1989) triangulated his study of a hospital rehabilitation center by using observation, questionnaires, and interviews. The latter two produced contradictory results. Duncan had inquired about heroes, for Deal and Kennedy (1982) write (and Duncan quotes, p. 232), "If values are the soul of the culture, then heroes personify those values and epitomize the strength of the organization." On a questionnaire, 70% of the respondents listed the director as a hero; her career demonstrated that one could be a fast-tracker in a public system that usually values longevity and loyalty more than performance or change. And 80% referred to the assistant director as a hero; he suffered from the same handicap as the center's clients and thus served as a role model and "a symbol to the employees of the special nature of their jobs" (Duncan, 1989, p. 232). In interviews, however, the same personnel insisted that "there are no heroes around here," including the director and assistant director.

"The questionnaire evidently provided respondents with an opportunity to make two points to themselves and others," writes Duncan (1989, p. 234). First, because personnel in rehabilitative settings need to feel that what they do is special, "the assistant director was a constant reminder to center employees that what they did *was* special; thus, he was a hero." Second, these employees had invested a great deal personally and financially to educate themselves. "Thus, they tried hard to convince themselves that fast tracking was possible, even within a large system that discouraged it. The director's success proved that fast trackers existed in their environment" (Duncan, 1989, p. 234). In interviews, however, center personnel "denied the importance of heroes in an attempt to convince the interviewer that everyone's contribution was equally important" (p. 234). Because they knew that the interviewer knew that promotions are rare, they described the director as an anomaly rather than a hero. "Center employees evidently wanted the interviewer to get the message that they all were professional, unconcerned with rank and status, and equally essential to the successful accomplishment of the organization's mission" (p. 234). On the questionnaire, respondents had said the center had a "work hard/play hard" or "you bet your organization" culture. They considered the hospital, not their own center, to be bureaucratic.

During the personal interviews, however, employees had to admit that the center was bureaucratic in order to support their belief that the center had no heroes. Thus, they could perpetuate an image of themselves as entrepreneurial professionals trapped in a system that allowed little innovation. They differentiated themselves from the hostile hospital environment by focusing on their cohesiveness, emphasizing the importance of their rituals and culture-building "staffings." (Duncan, 1989, p. 234)

In sum, the two data-gathering techniques evoked in members different, seemingly contradictory symbols; interpretations of themselves and others; and constructions of their organization. Questionnaire respondents viewed the hospital, not their own unit, as bureaucratic, and they presented the director as a symbol of the possibility of fast-tracking and the assistant director, who had suffered from the affliction treated by the rehab center, as a symbol of the program's success. When interviewed, however, they "wanted the interviewer *to get the message*" that all were equally essential to the unit's success; they reinterpreted the director's apparent fast-tracking as anomalous, reconstructed the unit as a bureaucracy "*to support their belief* that the center had no heroes," and created an *image* of themselves "trapped" in the system. Whatever else might be said about differences between quantitative and qualitative methods, the results reported here suggest that questionnaires and interviews are symbolic domains in which people respond with different symbols, beliefs, and interpretations, constructing themselves and their organization according to each framework. In other words, the tools of research in Duncan's study proved to be more than simply instruments, although this is how they are treated in manuals. These tools are symbolic; they convey meanings to the subjects of research who in turn respond to them as symbolic venues in which they behave symbolically, generating images, beliefs, and meanings appropriate to the context.

Symbolism in Science

Like the procedures used to gather data, the techniques of presenting research findings are both tools and symbolic forms. Although they advance knowledge and understanding, they do so through rhetorical conventions and strategies, stylistics, and symbols (Van Maanen, 1988, p. 5; Watson, 1995, pp. 305-306). Among the strategies are the four master tropes of metaphor, metonymy, synecdoche, and irony—the "stylistic means by which discourse constitutes the objects which it 'pretends' only to describe 'realistically' and analyze 'objectively' " (Manning, 1983, p. 227). Conventions comprise various rhetorical appeals that convey authority, authenticity, defensibility, and significance. John Van Maanen (1988) discusses three strategies of ethnographic writing and their conventions. *Realist tales* (the usual form of ethnographic reportage) establish authority by focusing on the people studied; in avoiding reference to the researchers, the accounts imply that it is the subjects' rather than the authors' perspective. *Confessional tales* are distinguished by "highly personalized styles and their self-absorbed mandates" (p. 73), and *impressionist tales* are dramatic recall that "mark and make memorable the fieldwork experience" (p. 102). Van Maanen illustrates the approaches with examples of his own writing.

Karen Golden-Biddle and Karen Locke (1993) also examine how ethnographic texts convince, focusing on the dimensions of authenticity, plausibility, and criticality. They compare and contrast three ethnographic articles in *Administrative Science Quarterly* (a sampling of the 14 published between 1979 and 1990): Adler and Adler (1988) on basketball teams, Barley (1983) on funeral homes, and Bartunek (1984) on a religious order. Symbols establishing authenticity (that the author was really "there" and also understands the data) include using local words and phrases; describing behaviors in detail; portraying what members think; indicating the length of stay, role, and context of the fieldwork; explicating the processes of data collection and analysis; and depicting a disciplined approach by using such expressions as "carefully," "as close as possible," "exact," and "careful and rigorous means." Ethnographers convey the plausibility of their interpretations in symbolic ways—for instance, through using schematics, diagrams, and other reductionistic forms "consistent with accepted scientific practice"; drafting the reader by referring to "we" and "us"; marshalling supporting witnesses or appealing to noted authorities; creating lacunae or gaps in the existing literature ("relatively few studies," "little is known about," etc.) that the author's work will fill; and building dramatic anticipation through the use of evocative language, which heightens the sense of discovery by projecting an image of the researcher on a quest ("searching," "looked," "seeking," "delved"). Criticality, or activating readers to reexamine assumptions in their own work, derives from tactics such as providing a "time out" in the text (such and such "should give one pause . . .") or urging the reader to imagine new possibilities (by using the subjunctive mode, e.g., "as if" and poetic devices such as metaphors).

Absence of conventions is as important symbolically as their inclusion. In *Tales of the Field: On Writing Ethnography,* Van Maanen (1988, p. 26) writes,

> Consider also the fullness of the empty sign. What is not in this book is as revealing as what is. There are no tables, charts, equations, pictures, inserts, underlinings, or joyless questions at the end of each chapter. This tells readers a good deal of what I think of them. . . . I have a pretty good idea of just who my readers are likely to be, and this influences what I write.

That scientific treatises and technical reports are symbolic expression is indicated by the many beliefs, personal experience narratives, and folk wisdom about how to appear credible and get published in a particular journal (see, e.g., Frost & Stablein, 1992). Photocopier lore satirizes the symbolics of science by offering a "key to scientific research literature" that contrasts what is said with what is meant (Dundes & Pagter, 1978, pp. 55-56; see also "technical writing kits" in the same source, pp. 56-58, and Brunvand, 1977, pp. 199-202): "It has long been known that" (i.e., "I haven't bothered to look up the original reference but . . ."), "Of great theoretical and practical importance . . ." (i.e., "Interesting to me"), "It is clear that much additional work will be required before a complete understanding . . ." (i.e., "I don't understand it"), and "Thanks are due to Joe Clotz for assistance with the experiments and to John Doe for valuable discussion" (i.e., "Clotz did the work and Doe explained what it meant"). Such "metacommunication" (Babcock, 1977) reveals that research, like other aspects of life, has a symbolic dimension.

Summary and Conclusion

When carrying out studies within organizations, field-workers present themselves symbolically to their subjects and are viewed as symbols, the techniques they employ to gather data are not just instruments but symbolic forms that produce different kinds of symbolism and meaning making, and their reports stand as symbols that also incorporate various symbolic devices affecting readers' responses. All this makes research itself an appropriate subject in the study of organizational symbolism.

Symbolism constructs and conveys meanings, evokes emotions, affects perceptions and beliefs, and influences actions. Organizational structure, technology, leadership, power, communication, and so on have a symbolic component (i.e., they are intended or inferred to convey meaning and significance beyond intrinsic content). Although some symbols are institutional (e.g., architecture, logos, company posters and slogans, annual reports, award ceremonies), much of symbolic behavior in organizations is folklore, that is, traditional expression learned and manifested as people interact with one another. This includes most examples of narrating, dress, rites of passage, rituals, customs, festive events, play, the use of proverbial speech, the personal decoration of workspace, and so on. Symbolism is often instrumental (or "functional")—for example, expressing values and norms for behavior, supporting social structure, creating a sense of common identity and community, contributing to organizational climate, helping individuals cope with uncertainty and ambiguity, and directing change. Symbols and symbolic behavior are the principal basis on which a group's culture is inferred. It is through symbolism that members construct organization and their understanding of it, which the symbolic interpretive approach seeks to document and present using qualitative methods that capture feelings, aesthetics, and meaning making occurring through symbolic performances in situated events. Reasons for studying organizational symbolism are to gain insights into the behavior of organizations and the people in them, to solve practical problems faced by organizations and their members, and even to better understand organizational science inasmuch as the researcher or consultant is a symbol and data-gathering techniques as well as presentations of findings have their symbolic dimension.

REFERENCES

Adler, P., & Adler, P. (1988). Intense loyalty in organizations: A case study of college athletics. *Administrative Science Quarterly, 33*, 401-417.

Alvesson, M., & Berg, P. (1992). *Corporate culture and organizational symbolism: Development, theoretical perspectives, practice and current debate.* Hawthorne, NY: Walter de Gruyter.

Applebaum, H. (1981). *Royal blue: The culture of construction.* New York: Holt, Rinehart and Winston.

Applebaum, H. (1987). Symbolic and humanistic anthropology: Introduction. In H. Applebaum (Ed.), *Perspectives in cultural anthropology* (pp. 477-487). Albany: State University of New York.

Arora, S. A. (1988). "No tickee, no shirtee": Proverbial speech in leadership and academe. In M. O. Jones, M. D. Moore, & R. C. Snyder (Eds.), *Inside organizations: Understanding the human dimension* (pp. 179-189). Newbury Park, CA: Sage.

Armstrong, R. P. (1971). *The affecting presence: An essay in humanistic anthropology.* Urbana: University of Illinois Press.

Babcock, B. A. (1977). The story in the story: Metanarration in folk narrative. In R. Bauman (Ed.), *Verbal art as performance* (pp. 61-79). Prospect Heights, IL: Waveland.

Barley, S. R. (1983). Semiotics and the study of occupational and organizational culture. *Administrative Science Quarterly, 23*, 393-413.

Barrett, F. J., & Cooperrider, D. L. (1990). Generative metaphor intervention: A new approach for working with systems divided by conflict and caught in defensive perception. *The Journal of Applied Behavioral Science, 26*, 219-239.

Bartunek, J. M. (1984). Changing interpretive schemes and organizational restructuring: The example of a religious order. *Administrative Science Quarterly, 9*, 355-372.

Bascom, W. R. (1954). Four functions of folklore. *Journal of American Folklore, 67*, 333-349.

Bauman, R. (1977). Verbal art as performance. In R. Bauman (Ed.), *Verbal art as performance* (pp. 3-58). Prospect Heights, IL: Waveland.

Bauman, R. (1986). *Story, performance, and event: Contextual studies of oral narratives.* New York: Cambridge University Press.

Beck, B. E. F., & Moore, L. F. (1985). Linking the host culture to organizational variables. In P. J. Frost, L. F. Moore, M. R. Louis, C. C. Lundberg, & J. Martin (Eds.), *Organizational culture* (pp. 335-353). Beverly Hills, CA: Sage.

Berg, P., & Kreiner, K. (1990). Corporate architecture: Turning physical settings into symbolic resources. In P. Gagliardi (Ed.), *Symbols and articles: Views of the corporate landscape* (pp. 41-67). New York: Aldine de Gruyter.

Bernard, H. R. (1988). *Research methods in cultural anthropology.* Newbury Park, CA: Sage.

Beyer, J. M., & Trice, H. M. (1988). The communication of power relations in organizations through cultural rites. In M. O. Jones, M. D. Moore, & R. C. Snyder (Eds.), *Inside organizations: Understanding the human dimension* (pp. 141-157). Newbury Park, CA: Sage.

Boje, D. M. (1991a). Consulting and change in the storytelling organization. *Journal of Organizational Change Management, 4*(3), 7-17.

Boje, D. M. (1991b). The storytelling organization: A study of story performance in an office-supply firm. *Administrative Science Quarterly, 36,* 106-126.

Briggs, C. L. (1986). *Learning how to ask: A sociolinguistic appraisal of the role of the interview in social science research.* Cambridge, NY: Cambridge University Press.

Bronner, S. J. (1986). *Grasping things: Folk material culture and mass society in America.* Lexington: University Press of Kentucky.

Brunvand, J. H. (1977). F.A.R.K. *Journal of American Folklore, 90,* 199-202.

Brunvand, J. H. (1978). *The study of American folklore: An introduction.* New York: W. W. Norton.

Burrell, G., & Morgan, G. (1979). *Sociological paradigms and organizational analysis.* London: Heinemann.

Caesar, W. (1975). "Asking a mouse who his favorite cat is": Musicians' stories about conductors. *Western Folklore, 34,* 83-116.

Cassirer, E. (1944). *An essay on man.* New Haven, CT: Yale University Press.

Chapple, E. O., & Coon, C. S. (1942). *Principles of anthropology.* New York: Holt.

Chase, G., & Reveal, E. C. (1983). *How to manage in the public sector.* Reading, MA: Addison-Wesley.

Christensen, D. (1988). Mirror, mission, and management: Reflections on folklore and culture in a health care organization. In M. O. Jones, M. D. Moore, & R. C. Snyder (Eds.), *Inside organizations: Understanding the human dimension* (pp. 49-61). Newbury Park, CA: Sage.

Clark, B. R. (1972). The organizational saga in higher education. *Administrative Science Quarterly, 17,* 178-184.

Cohen, A. (1976). *Two dimensional man: An essay on the anthropology of power and symbolism in complex society.* Berkeley: University of California Press.

Czarniawska-Joerges, B. (1992). *Exploring complex organizations: A cultural approach.* Newbury Park, CA: Sage.

Daft, R. L. (1983). Symbols in organizations: A dual-content framework of analysis. In L. R. Pondy, P. J. Frost, G. Morgan, & T. C. Dandridge (Eds.), *Organizational symbolism* (pp. 199-206). Greenwich, CT: JAI.

Dandridge, T. C. (1988). Work ceremonies: Why integrate work and play? In M. O. Jones, M. D. Moore, & R. C. Snyder (Eds.), *Inside organizations: Understanding the human dimension* (pp. 251-259). Newbury Park, CA: Sage.

Dandridge, T. C., Mitroff, I., & Joyce, W. F. (1980). Organizational symbolism: A topic to expand organizational analysis. *Academy of Management Review, 5,* 77-82.

Deal, T. E., & Kennedy, A. A. (1982). *Corporate cultures: The ritesand rituals of corporate life.* Reading, MA: Addison-Wesley.

Denzin, N. K. (1983). Interpretive interactionism. In G. Morgan (Ed.), *Beyond method* (pp. 129-146). Beverly Hills, CA: Sage.

Denzin, N. K. (1989). *Interpretive biography.* Newbury Park, CA: Sage.

Dewhurst, C. K. (1988). Art at work: In pursuit of aesthetic solutions. In M. O. Jones, M. D. Moore, & R. C. Snyder (Eds.), *Inside organizations: Understanding the human dimension* (pp. 245-250). Newbury Park, CA: Sage.

Dougherty, D., & Kunda, G. (1990). Photograph analysis: A method to capture organizational belief systems. In P. Gagliardi (Ed.), *Symbols and artifacts: Views of the corporate landscape* (pp. 185-206). New York: Aldine de Gruyter.

Doxtater, D. (1990). Meaning of the workplace: Using ideas of ritual space in design. In P. Gagliardi (Ed.), *Symbols and artifacts: Views of the corporate landscape* (pp. 107-127). New York: Aldine de Gruyter.

Duncan, W. J. (1989). Organizational culture: "Getting a fix" on an elusive concept. *The Academy of Management Executive, 3*(3), 229-236.

Dundes, A., & Pagter, C. (1978). *Urban folklore from the paperwork empire*. Bloomington: Indiana University Press.

Edgren, L. D. (1990). The "commando" model: A way to gather and interpret cultural data. In B. A. Turner (Ed.), *Organizational symbolism* (pp. 173-187). Berlin: Walter de Gruyter.

Ellis, B. (1987). Why are verbatim texts of legends necessary? In G. Bennett, P. Smith, & J. D. A. Widdowson (Eds.), *Perspectives on contemporary legend* (Vol. 2, pp. 31-60). Sheffield, UK: Sheffield Academic Press for Centre for English Cultural Tradition and Language.

Fetterman, D. M. (1989). *Ethnography step by step*. Newbury Park, CA: Sage.

Fine, E. C. (1984). *The folklore text: From performance to print*. Bloomington: Indiana University Press.

Forrest, J. (1988). *Lord I'm coming home: Everyday aesthetics in Tidewater North Carolina*. Ithaca, NY: Cornell University Press.

Fretz-Yoder, R. (1981). Mwanoka, a good storyteller, "pours on the oil." *Folklore and Mythology Studies, 5,* 20-33.

Frost, P., & Stablein, R. (Eds.). (1992). *Doing exemplary research*. Newbury Park, CA: Sage.

Gabriel, Y. (1991). Turning facts into stories and stories into facts: A hermeneutic exploration of organizational folklore. *Human Relations, 44,* 857-875.

Garson, B. (1975). *All the livelong day: The meaning and demeaning of routine work*. Garden City, NY: Doubleday.

Geertz, C. (1973). *The interpretation of cultures*. New York: Basic Books.

Georges, R. A. (1969). Toward an understanding of storytelling events. *Journal of American Folklore, 82,* 313-328.

Georges, R. A. (1979). Feedback and response in storytelling. *Western Folklore, 38,* 104-110.

Georges, R. A. (1981). Do narrators really digress? A reconsideration of "audience asides" in narrating. *Western Folklore, 40,* 245-252.

Georges, R. A. (1983). The universality of the tale-type as concept and construct. *Western Folklore, 42,* 21-28.

Georges, R. A. (1987). Timeliness and appropriateness in personal experience narrating. *Western Folklore, 46,* 115-120.

Georges, R. A. (1990). Communicative role and social identity in storytelling. *Fabula, 31,* 49-57.

Georges, R. A. (1994). The concept of "repertoire" in folkloristics. *Western Folklore, 53,* 313-323.

Georges, R. A. (1995, May). *Pervasive and persistent misconceptions about storytelling*. Unpublished paper presented at A Conference Exploring the Role of Storytelling in Contemporary America, University of California, Los Angeles.

Georges, R. A., & Jones, M. O. (1980). *People studying people: The human element in fieldwork*. Berkeley: University of California Press.

66

Georges, R. A., & Jones, M. O. (1995). *Folkloristics: An introduction*. Bloomington: Indiana University Press.

Gherardi, S. (1995). When will he say: "Today the plates are soft"? The management of ambiguity and situated decision-making. *Studies in Cultures, Organizations and Societies, 1,* 9-27.

Goffman, I. (1959). *The presentation of self in everyday life*. Garden City, NY: Doubleday.

Golden-Biddle, K., & Locke, K. (1993). Appealing work: An investigation of how ethnographic texts convince. *Organization Science, 4,* 595-616.

Goldstein, K. S. (1964). *A guide for field workers in folklore*. Hatboro, PA: Folklore Associates.

Harris, S. G., & Sutton, R. I. (1986). Functions of parting ceremonies in dying organizations. *Academy of Management Journal, 29,* 5-30.

Hatch, M. J. (1993a). The dynamics of organizational culture. *Academy of Management Review, 18,* 657-693.

Hatch, M. J. (1993b, August). *Reading irony in the humor of a management team: Organizational contradictions in context*. Unpublished paper presented at the meeting of the Academy of Management, Las Vegas, NV.

Hatch, M. J., & Ehrlich, S. B. (1993). Where there is smoke: Spontaneous humor as an indicator of paradox and ambiguity in organizations. *Organization Studies, 14,* 505-526.

Hatch, M. J., & Jones, M. O. (1994, July). *Humor, history, continuity: Tempting organizational analysts with photocopier lore*. Unpublished paper presented at SCOS (Standing Committee on Organizational Symbolism), Calgary.

Henry, P. J. (1988). *The role of war stories in organizational culture*. Doctoral dissertation, Communications Studies, University of Iowa.

Hirschhorn, L. (1988). *The workplace within: The psychodynamics of organizational life*. Cambridge, MA: MIT Press.

Höpfl, H., & Linstead, S. (1993). Passion and performance: Suffering and the carrying of organizational roles. In S. Fineman (Ed.), *Emotions in organizations* (pp. 76-93). Newbury Park, CA: Sage.

Ives, E. D. (1980). *The tape-recorded interview: A manual for field workers in folklore and oral history*. Knoxville: University of Tennessee Press.

Jackson, B. (1987). *Fieldwork*. Urbana: University of Illinois Press.

Jick, T. J. (1983). Mixing qualitative and quantitative methods: Triangulation in action. In J. Van Maanen (Ed.), *Qualitative methodology* (pp. 135-148). Beverly Hills, CA: Sage.

Jones, M. O. (1984). Works of art, art as work, and the arts of working: Implications for the study of organizational life. *Western Folklore, 43,* 172-221.

Jones, M. O. (1987). *Exploring folk art: Twenty years of thought on craft, work, and aesthetics*. Ann Arbor, MI: UMI Research Press. (Reprinted Logan: Utah State University Press, 1993)

Jones, M. O. (1988). In search of meaning: Using qualitative methods in research and application. In M. O. Jones, M. D. Moore, & R. C. Snyder (Eds.), *Inside organizations: Understanding the human dimension* (pp. 31-47). Newbury Park, CA: Sage.

Jones, M. O. (1990). A folklore approach to emotions in work. *American Behavioral Scientist, 33,* 278-286.

Jones, M. O. (1991a). On fieldwork, symbols, and folklore in the writings of William Foote Whyte. In P. J. Frost, L. F. Moore, M. R. Louis, C. C. Lundberg, & J. Martin (Eds.), *Reframing organizational culture* (pp. 192-204). Newbury Park, CA: Sage.

Jones, M. O. (1991b). What if stories don't tally with the culture? *Journal of Organizational Change Management, 4*(3), 27-34.

Jones, M. O. (1991c). Why folklore and organization(s)? *Western Folklore, 50,* 29-40.

Jones, M. O. (1994). A folkloristic approach to organizational behavior (OB) and organization development (OD). In M. O. Jones (Ed.), *Putting folklore to use* (pp. 162-186). Lexington: University Press of Kentucky.

Jones, M. O. (in press). How can we apply event analysis to "material behavior," and why should we? *Folklore and Mythology Studies.*

Jorgensen, D. L. (1989). *Participant observation: A methodology for human studies.* Newbury Park, CA: Sage.

Kaplan, A. (1964). *The conduct of inquiry: Methodology for behavioral science.* San Francisco: Chandler.

Kanter, R. (1977). *Men and women of the corporation.* New York: Basic Books.

Kirk, J., & Miller, M. L. (1986). *Reliability and validity in qualitative research.* Beverly Hills, CA: Sage.

Kirshenblatt-Gimblett, B. (1989). Objects of memory: Material culture as life review. In E. Oring (Ed.), *Folk groups and folklore genres: A reader* (pp. 329-338). Logan: Utah State University Press.

Kluckhohn, F. (1940). The participant-observer technique in small communities. *American Journal of Sociology, 46,* 331-343.

Kroeber, A. L., & Kluckhohn, C. (1952). *Culture: A critical review of concepts and definitions.* New York: Vintage.

Kunda, G. (1992). *Engineering culture: Control and commitment in a high tech corporation.* Philadelphia: Temple University Press.

Larsen, J., & Schultz, M. (1990). Artifacts within a bureaucratic monastery. In P. Gagliardi (Ed.), *Symbols and artifacts: Views of the corporate landscape* (pp. 281-302). New York: Aldine de Gruyter.

Lockwood, Y. R. (1984). The joy of labor. *Western Folklore, 43,* 202-211.

Lofland, J. (1971). *Analyzing social settings: A guide to qualitative observations and analysis.* Belmont, CA: Wadsworth.

Louis, M. (1980). Surprise and sense making: What newcomers experience in entering unfamiliar organization settings. *Administrative Science Quarterly, 25,* 226-251.

Louis, M. (1983). Organizations as cultural-bearing milieux. In L. R. Pondy, P. J. Frost, G. Morgan, & T. C. Dandridge (Eds.), *Organizational symbolism* (pp. 39-54). Greenwich, CT: JAI.

MacIver, R. M. (1942). *Social causation.* New York: Ginn and Co.

Manning, P. K. (1983). Metaphors of the field: Varieties of organizational discourse. In J. Van Maanen (Ed.), *Qualitative methodology.* Beverly Hills, CA: Sage.

Martin, J., & Powers, M. E. (1983). Truth or corporate propaganda: The value of a good war story. In L. R. Pondy, P. J. Frost, G. Morgan, & T. C. Dandridge (Eds.), *Organizational symbolism* (pp. 93-107). Greenwich: JAI.

McCall, M. M. (1990). The significance of storytelling. *Studies in Symbolic Interaction, 11,* 145-161.

68

Meyerson, D. E. (1990). Uncovering socially undesirable emotions: Experiences of ambiguity in organizations. *American Behavioral Scientist, 33,* 296-307.

Moch, M., & Huff, A. S. (1982). Life on the line. *The Wharton Magazine, 6*(4), 53-58.

Moch, M., & Huff, A. S. (1983). "Chewing ass out": The enactment of power relationships through language and ritual. *Journal of Business Research, 11,* 293-316.

Moore, M. D. (1988). Resolving conflict and establishing community: The annual festival "Old People's Day." In M. O. Jones, M. D. Moore, & R. C. Snyder (Eds.), *Inside organizations: Understanding the human dimension* (pp. 261-269). Newbury Park, CA: Sage.

Morgan, G. (1986). *Images of organization.* Beverly Hills, CA: Sage.

Morgan, G., Frost, P. J., & Pondy, L. R. (1983). Organizational symbolism. In L. R. Pondy, P. J. Frost, G. Morgan, & T. C. Dandridge (Eds.), *Organizational symbolism* (pp. 3-35). Greenwich, CT: JAI.

Musello, C. (1992). Objects in process: Material culture and communication. *Southern Folklore, 49,* 37-59.

Narasimhan, A., & Pillutla, M. M. (1994, August). *Comic texts: A critical hermeneutic understanding of office-door cartoon displays.* Unpublished paper presented at the meeting of the Academy of Management, Dallas, TX.

Narváez, P. (1990). "I've gotten soppy": "Send-off parties" as rites of passage in the occupational folklife of CBC reporters. *American Behavioral Scientist, 33,* 339-352.

Nickerson, B. (1976). *Industrial lore: A study of an urban factory.* Doctoral dissertation, Folklore, Indiana University.

Nickerson, B. (1983). Factory folklore. In R. M. Dorson (Ed.), *Handbook of American folklore* (pp. 121-127). Bloomington: Indiana University Press.

Nickerson, B. (1990). Antagonism at work: Them and us, a widget world view. *American Behavioral Scientist, 33,* 308-317.

Noon, M., & Delbridge, R. (1993). News from behind my hand: Gossip in organizations. *Organization Studies, 14,* 23-36.

Olrik, A. (1909). Epische Gesetze der Volksdichtung [Epic laws of folk narrative]. *Zeitschrift für Deutsches Altertum [Journal for German Antiquity],* 51, 1-12. (Reprinted in *The study of folklore,* pp. 129-141, by A. Dundes, Ed., 1965, Englewood Cliffs, NJ: Prentice Hall.)

Ott, J. S. (1989). *The organizational culture perspective.* Pacific Grove, CA: Brooks/Cole.

Patton, M. Q. (1990). *Qualitative evaluation and research methods* (2nd ed.). Newbury Park, CA: Sage.

Peters, T. J. (1978, Autumn). Symbols, patterns and settings: An optimistic case for getting things done. *Organizational Dynamics,* pp. 3-27.

Peters, T. J., & Waterman, R. H., Jr. (1982). *In search of excellence: Lessons from America's best-run companies.* New York: Harper and Row.

Pondy, L. R., Frost, P. J., Morgan, G., & Dandridge, T. C. (Eds.). (1983). *Organizational symbolism.* Greenwich, CT: JAI.

Prasad, P. (1993). Symbolic processes in the implementation of technological change: A symbolic interactionist study of work computerization. *Academy of Management Journal, 36,* 1400-1429.

Radcliffe-Brown, A. R. (1935). On the concept of function in social science. *American Anthropologist, 37,* 394-402.

Rafaeli, A., & Pratt, M. G. (1993). Tailored meanings: On the meaning and impact of organizational dress. *Academy of Management Review, 18,* 32-55.

Raspa, R. (1989). Folkloric expression in the automobile industry. *Southern Folklore, 46,* 71-78.

Riessman, C. K. (1993). *Narrative analysis.* Newbury Park, CA: Sage.

Rose, A. M. (1962). *Human behavior and social processes: An interactionist approach.* Boston: Houghton Mifflin.

Rossi, I. (1980). Introduction. In I. Rossi (Ed.), *People in culture* (pp. 1-28). New York: Praeger.

Roy, D. (1959-1960). Banana time: Job satisfaction and informal interaction. *Human Organization, 18,* 158-168.

Sackmann, S. A. (1989). The role of metaphors in organization transformation. *Human Relations, 42,* 463-485.

Sackmann, S. A. (1991). *Cultural knowledge in organizations: Exploring the collective mind.* Newbury Park, CA: Sage.

Sanday, P. R. (1983). The ethnographic paradigm(s). In J. Van Maanen (Ed.), *Qualitative methodology* (pp. 19-36). Beverly Hills, CA: Sage.

Santino, J. (1978a). Characteristics of occupational narrative. *Western Folklore, 38,* 57-70.

Santino, J. (1978b). *The outlaw emotions: Workers' narratives from three contemporary occupations.* Doctoral dissertation, Folklore and Folklife, University of Pennsylvania.

Santino, J. (1990). The outlaw emotions: Narrative expressions on the rules and roles of occupational identity. *American Behavioral Scientist, 33,* 318-329.

Scheiberg, S. L. (1990). Emotions on display: The personal decoration of work space. *American Behavioral Scientist, 33,* 330-338.

Scheid-Cook, T. L. (1988). Mitigating organizational contradictions: The role of mediatory myths. *The Journal of Applied Behavioral Science, 24,* 161-171.

Schein, E. H. (1985). *Organizational culture and leadership: A dynamic view.* San Francisco: Jossey-Bass.

Schultz, M. (1991). Transitions between symbolic domains in organizations. *Organization Studies, 12,* 489-506.

Schultz, M. (1994). *On studying organizational cultures: Diagnosis and understanding.* New York: Walter de Gruyter.

Schwartzman, H. B. (1988). Stories at work: Play in an organizational context. In E. M. Bruner (Ed.), *Text, play and story: The construction and reconstruction of self and society* (pp. 80-93). Prospect Heights, IL: Waveland.

Schwartzman, H. B. (1989). *The meeting: Gatherings in organizations and communities.* New York: Plenum.

Schwartzman, H. B. (1993). *Ethnography in organizations.* Newbury Park, CA: Sage.

Siehl, C., & Martin, J. (1988). Measuring organizational culture: Mixing qualitative and quantitative methods. In M. O. Jones, M. D. Moore, & R. C. Snyder (Eds.), *Inside organizations: Understanding the human dimension* (pp. 79-103). Newbury Park, CA: Sage.

Smircich, L. (1983a). Concepts of culture and organizational analysis. *Administrative Science Quarterly, 28,* 339-358.

Smircich, L. (1983b). Studying organizations as cultures. In G. Morgan (Ed.), *Beyond method* (pp. 160-172). Beverly Hills, CA: Sage.

Smircich, L. (1985). Is the concept of culture a paradigm for understanding organizations and ourselves? In P. J. Frost, L. F. Moore, M. R. Louis, C. C. Lundberg, & J. Martin (Eds.), *Organizational culture* (pp. 55-72). Beverly Hills, CA: Sage.

70

Smircich, L., & Calás, M. B. (1987). Organizational culture: A critical assessment. In F. M. Jablin, L. L. Putnam, K. H. Roberts, & L. W. Porter (Eds.), *Handbook of organizational communication: An interdisciplinary perspective* (pp. 228-263). Newbury Park, CA: Sage.

Sonduck, M. M., & Perry, B. (1983, November). *Anecdotal survey feedback: Expanding the range of OD technology.* Unpublished paper presented at the meeting of the Organization Development Network, Pasadena, CA.

Spradley, J. B. (1979). *The ethnographic interview.* New York: Holt, Rinehart and Winston.

Spradley, J. B. (1980). *Participant observation.* New York: Holt, Rinehart and Winston.

Spradley, J. B., & McCurdy, D. W. (1972). *The cultural experience: Ethnography in a complex society.* Chicago: Science Research Associates.

Stahl, S. K. D. (1977). The personal narrative as folklore. *Journal of the Folklore Institute, 14,* 9-30.

Stahl, S. K. D. (1989). *Literary folkloristics and the personal narrative.* Bloomington: Indiana University Press.

Stanley, D. H. (1977). Play and performance in *Enkai,* the Japanese corporate drinking party. *Folklore Annual of the University [of Texas] Folklore Association, 7-8,* 1-11.

Steele, F. I. (1973). *Physical settings and organizational development.* Reading, MA: Addison-Wesley.

Stephenson, K. A. (1990). *Emerging corporate groups: A study of institutional processes in a technical setting.* Doctoral dissertation, Anthropology, Harvard University.

Strati, A. (1990). Aesthetics and organizational skill. In B. A. Turner (Ed.), *Organizational symbolism* (pp. 208-222). Berlin: Walter de Gruyter.

Strati, A. (1992). Aesthetic understanding of organizational life. *Academy of Management Review, 17,* 568-581.

Strati, A. (1995). Aesthetics and organizations without walls. *Studies in Cultures, Organizations and Societies, 1,* 83-105.

Thoms, W. (1965). Folklore. In A. Dundes (Ed.), *The study of folklore* (pp. 4-6). Englewood Cliffs, NJ: Prentice Hall.

Toelken, B. (1979). *The dynamics of folklore.* Boston: Houghton Mifflin.

Tommerup, P. (1990). Stories about an inspiring leader: "Rapture" and the symbolics of employee fulfillment. *American Behavioral Scientist, 33,* 374-385.

Tommerup, P. (1993). *Adhocratic traditions, experience narratives and personal transformation: An ethnographic study of the organizational culture and folklore of The Evergreen State College, an innovative liberal arts college.* Doctoral dissertation, Folklore and Mythology, University of California, Los Angeles.

Traweek, S. (1988). *Beamtimes and lifetimes: The world of high energy physicists.* Cambridge, MA: Harvard University Press.

Trice, H. M. (1993). *Occupational subcultures in the workplace.* Ithaca, NY: LRL Press, Cornell University.

Trice, H. M., & Beyer, J. M. (1984). Studying organizational cultures through rites and ceremonials. *Academy of Management Review, 9,* 653-669.

Trice, H. M., & Beyer, J. M. (1992). *The cultures of work organizations.* Englewood Cliffs, NJ: Prentice Hall.

Trice, H. M., Belasco, J., & Alutto, J. A. (1969). The role of ceremonials in organizational behavior. *Industrial and Labor Relations Review, 23,* 40-51.

Turner, B. A. (1990a). Introduction. In B. A. Turner (Ed.), *Organizational symbolism* (pp. 1-11). Hawthorne, NY: Walter de Gruyter.

Turner, B. A. (1990b). The rise of organizational symbolism. In J. Hassard & D. Pym (Eds.), *The theory and philosophy of organizations: Critical issues and new perspectives* (pp. 83-96). London: Routledge.

Turner, B. A. (1992). The symbolic understanding of organizations. In M. Reed & M. Hughes (Eds.), *Rethinking organization: New directions in organization theory and analysis* (pp. 46-66). Newbury Park, CA: Sage.

Tylor, E. B. (1958). *The origins of culture* (Part I of *Primitive culture*). New York: Harper & Row. (Original publication 1871).

Ulrich, W. L. (1984). HRM and culture: History, ritual, and myth. *Human Resource Management, 23,* 117-128.

Vance, C. M. (1991). Formalizing storytelling in organizations: A key agenda for the design of training. *Journal of Organizational Change Management, 4*(3), 52-48.

Van Maanen, J. (1982). Fieldwork on the beat. In J. Van Maanen, J. M. Dabbs, Jr., & R. R. Faulkner (Eds.), *Varieties of qualitative research* (pp. 103-151). Beverly Hills, CA: Sage.

Van Maanen, J. (1983). The fact of fiction in organizational ethnography. In J. Van Maanen (Ed.), *Qualitative methodology* (pp. 37-55). Beverly Hills, CA: Sage.

Van Maanen, J. (1988). *Tales of the field: On writing ethnography.* Chicago: University of Chicago Press.

Van Maanen, J. (1991). Playing back the tape: Early days in the field. In W. B. Shaffir & R. A. Stebbins (Eds.), *Experiencing fieldwork: An inside view of qualitative research* (pp. 31-42). Newbury Park, CA: Sage.

Van Maanen, J., & Barley, S. R. (1984). Occupational communities: Culture and control in organizations. *Research in Organizational Behavior, 6,* 287-365.

Van Maanen, J., & Kunda, G. (1989). "Real feelings": Emotional expression and organizational culture. *Research in Organizational Behavior, 11,* 43-104.

von Sydow, C. W. (1948). *Selected papers on folklore* (L. Bodker, Ed.). Copenhagen: Rosenkilde and Bagger. (Reprinted in 1977 by Arno Press, New York)

Wambaugh, J. (1975). *The choirboys.* New York: Delacorte.

Watson, T. J. (1995). Shaping the story: Rhetoric, persuasion and creative writing in organizational ethnography. *Studies in Cultures, Organizations and Societies, 1,* 301-311.

Werner, O., & Schoepfle, G. M. (1987). *Systematic fieldwork: Vol. 1. Foundations of ethnography and interviewing.* Newbury Park, CA: Sage.

Westley, F. R. (1990). The eye of the needle: Cultural and personal transformation in a traditional organization. *Human Relations, 43,* 273-293.

White, L. A. (1949). *The science of culture, a study of man and civilization.* New York: Farrar, Straus and Giroux.

Whyte, W. F. (1953). Interviewing for organizational research. *Human Organization, 12*(2), 15-22.

Whyte, W. F. (1957). On asking indirect questions. *Human Organization, 15,* 21-23.

Whyte, W. F. (1961). *Men at work.* Homewood, IL: Dorsey Press and Richard D. Irwin.

Whyte, W. F. (1984). *Learning from the field: A guide from experience.* Beverly Hills, CA: Sage.

Wilkins, A. L. (1979). *Organizational stories as an expression of management philosophy: Implications for social control in organizations.* Unpublished doctoral dissertation, Organizational Behavior, Stanford University, CA.

Wilkins, A. L. (1984). The creation of company cultures: The role of stories and human resource systems. *Human Resource Management, 23,* 41-60.

Wilkins, A. L., & Thompson, M. P. (1991). On getting the story crooked (and straight). *Journal of Organizational Change Management, 4,* 18-26.

Wilson, W. A. (1988). Dealing with organizational stress: Lessons from the folklore of Mormon missionaries. In M. O. Jones, M. D. Moore, & R. C. Snyder (Eds.), *Inside organizations: Understanding the human dimension* (pp. 271-280). Newbury Park, CA: Sage.

Witkin, R. W. (1990a). The aesthetic imperative of a rational-technical machinery: A study in organizational control through the design of artifacts. In P. Gagliardi (Ed.), *Symbols and artifacts: Views of the corporate landscape* (pp. 325-338). New York: Aldine de Gruyter.

Witkin, R. W. (1990b). The collusive manoeuvre: A study of organizational style in work relations. In B. A. Turner (Ed.), *Organizational symbolism* (pp. 191-205). Berlin: Aldine de Gruyter.

Witkin, R. W., & Poupart, R. (1986). Running a commentary on imaginatively re-lived events: A method for obtaining qualitatively rich data. In A. Strati (Ed.), *The symbolics of skill* (pp. 79-87). Trento, Italy: University of Trento, Dipartimento di Politica Socials.

Yanow, D. J. (1994, July). *Space stories: Constructing and telling the public past, present, and/or hoped-for future.* Unpublished paper presented at the meeting of the SCOS (Standing Committee on Organizational Symbolism), Calgary.

Young, K. G. (1987). *Taleworlds and storyrealms: The phenomenology of narrative.* Dordrecht, The Netherlands: Martinus Nijhoff.

Zuboff, S. (1988). *In the age of the smart machines: The future of work and power.* New York: Basic Books.

ABOUT THE AUTHOR

MICHAEL OWEN JONES is Professor of Folklore and History at the University of California, Los Angeles. He has a B.A. in History, Art, and International Relations from the University of Kansas and an M.A. in Folklore and a Ph.D. in Folklore and American Studies from Indiana University. He is author or editor of 10 books and more than 100 articles and review essays on organizational symbolism and folklore, fieldwork, film and folklore, folk art, food customs and symbolism, folk medicine, and research methods. He is also general editor of a series of books on folk art and artists with the University Press of Mississippi, and he has edited a volume of *American Behavioral Scientist* (vol. 33) on "Emotions in Work." Among his books are *People Studying People: The Human Element in Fieldwork* (co-authored); *Inside Organizations: Understanding the Human Dimension* (co-edited); *Exploring Folk Art: Twenty Years of Thought on Craft, Work, and Aesthetics; Craftsman of the Cumberlands: Tradition and Creativity; Putting Folklore to Use* (edited); and *Folkloristics: An Introduction* (co-authored).

Qualitative Research Methods

Series Editor
JOHN VAN MAANEN
Massachusetts Institute of Technology

Associate Editors:
Peter K. Manning, *Michigan State University*
& Marc L. Miller, *University of Washington*

Other volumes in this series listed on outside back cover